Higher
Computing
Science

Practice Papers for SQA Exams

David Alford

Contents

HODDER
GIBSON
AN HACHETTE UK COMPANY

The Publishers would like to thank the following for permission to reproduce copyright material:

Acknowledgements

Exam rubrics in Section 1 and Section 2 of each practice paper Copyright © Scottish Qualifications Authority.

Every effort has been made to trace all copyright holders, but if any have been inadvertently overlooked, the Publishers will be pleased to make the necessary arrangements at the first opportunity.

Although every effort has been made to ensure that website addresses are correct at time of going to press, Hodder Gibson cannot be held responsible for the content of any website mentioned in this book. It is sometimes possible to find a relocated web page by typing in the address of the home page for a website in the URL window of your browser.

Hachette UK's policy is to use papers that are natural, renewable and recyclable products and made from wood grown in sustainable forests. The logging and manufacturing processes are expected to conform to the environmental regulations of the country of origin.

Orders: please contact Bookpoint Ltd, 130 Park Drive, Milton Park, Abingdon, Oxon OX14 4SE. Telephone: (44) 01235 827720. Fax: (44) 01235 400401. Email education@bookpoint.co.uk. Lines are open from 9 a.m. to 5 p.m., Monday to Saturday, with a 24-hour message answering service. Visit our website at www.hoddereducation.co.uk. Hodder Gibson can also be contacted directly at hoddergibson@hodder.co.uk

Cover photo © crstrbrt/123RF.com
Illustrations by Aptara Inc.
Typeset in Din Regular 12/14.4 pt. by Aptara Inc.
Printed in the UK

A catalogue record for this title is available from the British Library.

ISBN: 978 1 5104 1353 5

Introduction

Higher Computing Science

The course

Prerequisite knowledge

Before sitting this course, it is expected that you will have passed National 5 Computing Science. The content of Higher Computing Science will build upon the skills and knowledge gained at National 5 level.

Higher Computing Science units

The two unit assessments will be mandatory up until and including the 2017–18 session. After this, unit content will still be covered in the course, but will be assessed in the Assignment and Question Paper. Teachers may decide to have candidates undertake unit assessments at their discretion.

The Assignment

In session 2017–18, the Assignment will be worth 60 marks. This is 40 per cent of the overall available marks. This will be combined with a 90-mark question paper to give a total of 150 available marks.

From session 2018–19 onwards, there will be changes to the number of marks available within the Assignment and the Question Paper. The exact nature of these changes has yet to be decided by SQA. However, if SQA chooses to follow the pattern of the changes made to the National 5 Computing Science course, then the Assignment will be worth 50 marks (31 per cent of the overall available marks) combined with a 110-mark question paper, to give a total of 160 available marks.

The Assignment will require you to show your understanding and skills in the following areas:

- analysis of a problem
- program design
- information system design
- writing program code
- creation of an information system
- scripting within an information system
- evaluation of your solution.

The question paper

The question paper will assess your problem-solving ability, making reference to technical knowledge in the areas stated within the Course Assessment Specification. This document can be accessed for free from the Higher Computing Science section of the SQA website, under Course Assessment Specification.

The question paper brief can also be accessed for free from the Higher Computing Science section of the SQA website, under Specimen Question Papers and Marking Instructions. This document indicates how many marks within the question paper will be assigned to each area.

Where questions involve a candidate interpreting program code, the code will be in SQA Reference Language. Candidates are not required to answer in SQA Reference Language; only to read and understand it. The full specification for SQA Reference Language can be accessed for free from the Higher Computing Science section of the SQA website, under Reference Language.

The current format of the question paper consists of 90 marks.

Section 1 will consist of individual problem-solving questions and is worth a total of 20 marks.

Section 2 will consist of longer, scenario-based problem-solving questions and is worth a total of 70 marks.

How to use this book

This book can be used in two ways.

1   You can complete an entire practice paper under examination conditions, without reference to books or notes, and then mark your answers using the answers provided. This will give you a clear indication of the level at which you are currently working, and enable you to target any areas of content in which you need to improve.

2   You can complete a practice paper using your notes and books. Try a question first, and then refer to the answers section to ensure you have sufficient detail to gain all the available marks. If you are unable to answer a question, or discover your answer was not to the required standard, you should refer to your notes and books.

The revision grid provided allows you to target a specific area of content should you require practice on a specific topic.

Hints and tips

Below is a list of hints and tips that will help you in your SQA examination paper.

- Make sure you read each question carefully. The detail in the question sets the scene for the problem to be solved.
- Refer to the situation described in the question. The papers are designed to test how a candidate applies their knowledge to a situation.
- Use technical terms. A Higher-level answer will require certain terms from the course to be used.
- No marks will be given for repeating information given in the question. You can and should refer to the question, but build on that with the points you wish to make in order to gain the marks.
- Include as much detail as you can. As you will see from the answers provided, many questions have multiple possible answers. If a marker deems that you lack enough technical detail to give you a mark on one point, they can still give you the mark for a separate fully explained point. As much as possible, SQA markers undertake positive marking. This means if a question is worth 2 marks, and a candidate makes one wrong point and two correct points, they will be awarded the 2 marks.

- When doing questions involving calculations, show all your working. If you make a small mistake under pressure, you will still gain some of the available marks.
- Ensure you have a scientific calculator with you in the examination.
- Attempt all questions. Leaving an answer blank means you will definitely receive no marks for it.
- Some candidates will have used programming languages where arrays are indexed beginning with element[1]. In SQA exams, arrays are indexed from zero, not one.
- Access the Course Assessment Specification from the Higher Computing Science section of the SQA website to guide your revision.

Remember sometimes your biggest resource is people. Speak to your teacher about any concerns that you have, support your classmates and enjoy their support in return. Good luck realising your potential in Higher Computing Science.

Key Area index grids

Key area	Paper A		Paper B		Paper C		Date to complete
	Section 1	Section 2	Section 1	Section 2	Section 1	Section 2	
Software Design and Development							
Languages and environments	4	17b)	8		4	15a)	
Computational constructs		17d), 17e)		13a), 13d), 13e)	2	12b)	
Data types and structures		11a), 11b), 11c)	9a), 9b)			12a), 12b)	
Testing and documenting solutions		14d)		11c), 11d), 13c)		15b), 16d)	
Algorithm specification	8	14e)		11a), 13b)		12b), 13a), 15c)	
Low-level operations and computer architecture	1, 2, 3	15b), 15c), 17c), 18a), 18c)	1, 3, 10	14f), 14g), 15b) (ii)	1, 3	14g) (ii), 15d), 16a)	
Software and Information System Design and Development							
Design notations		12a), 12b)		12a)		14b), 16b)	
Development methodologies	5	14a), 14c), 17a)	2			16c), 16f)	
Contemporary developments		13d)		11e)		14g) (i)	
User interface		16d)	7		9		
Information System Design and Development							
Structures and links (database)	9a), 9b)	12c), 12d)		12b)		14a), 14c), 14d)	
Structures and links (web-based)		13a), 13b)		12d), 12e), 15c)	8, 10	13c), 13d)	
Media types	7a), 7b)			15a), 15b) (i)	11	13g) (i), 13h)	
Coding		16a), 16b)		12c), 14b), 14c)		13c)	
Testing		11e), 18d)		14a)		14f), 16e), 16g)	
Purpose, functionality, users		12c)				13d), 13e)	

Key area	Paper A		Paper B		Paper C		Date to complete
	Section 1	Section 2	Section 1	Section 2	Section 1	Section 2	
Technical Implementation (hardware requirements)		18a)	4		6		
Technical Implementation (software requirements)		14b), 15a)		11b), 15d)		13g) (iii)	
Technical implementation (storage)	10a), 10b)			14d), 14e)		13f), 13g) (ii), 14e)	
Technical implementation (networking/ connectivity)	6a), 6b)			12e)			
Security risks		16c)	5				
Security precautions		16e)	6a), 6b)			13b)	
Legal implications		13c)					
Environmental implications		13d), 18b)				16h)	
Economic and social impact		11d), 13d)			5, 7		

Higher
Computing
Science

Duration: 2 hours

Total marks: 90

Section 1 – 20 marks

Attempt ALL questions.

Section 2 – 70 marks

Attempt ALL questions.

Show all workings.

In the exam you must write your answers in the answer booklet provided and clearly identify the question number you are attempting.

Use **blue** or **black** ink.

Section 1

MARKS

1 Convert the decimal number −92 into binary using 8-bit two's complement.

1

_____

2 Kevin has written a program that involves storing text files. Give **one** reason why the use of Unicode might be preferable to ASCII for storage of text.

1

_____

_____

3 Reece wishes to store a video clip that has a frame rate of 30 frames per second, a duration of 11 seconds and a resolution of 1920 × 1080 with a colour depth of 8 bits. Calculate the storage requirement for the uncompressed video clip. Show all working and express your answer in appropriate units.

2

4 Lesley is writing an object-oriented program. Inheritance by subclasses from parent classes is a key feature of object oriented programming. Explain how inheritance is an advantage to Lesley.

2

_____

_____

_____

_____

5 BamfTech are undertaking analysis of a new problem submitted by a client. In the software development process, describe the activities undertaken at the analysis stage.

2

_____

_____

_____

_____

_____

_____

6 Anne manages a local area network that was set up for a small business. The network currently makes use of hub.

a) Describe how a hub transmits data on a network.

1

_____

_____

As the business expands and more devices are being added to the network, Anne is considering removing the hub and instead installing a switch.

b) Explain how using a switch in place of a hub can improve network performance.

2

_____

_____

_____

_____

7 MP3 is a lossy compression format commonly used for audio.

a) Describe what is meant by lossy compression.

1

_____

MP3 makes use of perceptual coding to compress audio data.

b) Describe **one** technique used in perceptual coding to compress sound.

_____

_____

1

8 Briony works for a delivery company. She has written an algorithm that will search for a target ID code from a list of 18 parcels. Each parcel has a unique parcel ID code, stored in the array named `parcel_code( )`. Part of the algorithm is shown below.

Line 1   `SET found TO false`

Line 2   `RECEIVE target_code FROM KEYBOARD`

Line 3   `FOR iteration = 0 TO 17`

Line 4   _____

Line 5   `SET found = true`

Line 6   `END IF`

Line 7   `NEXT iteration`

What command should be in line 4?

_____

_____

1

9 Landon works in the office at Longlees Primary School. He issues passes to staff at the school using the form below:

STAFF	
Forename	Alan
Surname	Prentice
Designation	Teacher

A staff member's designation can be one of 'Teacher', 'Office', 'Janitor', 'Kitchen', 'Classroom Assistant' or 'Cleaner'.

a) Landon uses a compound key for this database. Explain what a compound key is and why this might lead to problems in this situation.

_____

_____

_____

_____

2

b) Landon decides to add a surrogate key to eliminate the potential problems. Explain how Landon would add a surrogate key.

1

_____

_____

10 Vera runs a dental surgery, and is thinking about storing patients' personal, medical and payment data using offline storage.

a) Describe **one** advantage of offline storage in this situation.

1

_____

_____

_____

A colleague recommends that Vera use a public cloud instead for the storage of patients' personal, medical and payment data.

b) Describe **one** advantage and **one** disadvantage of using a public cloud in this situation.

2

_____

_____

_____

_____

_____

_____

[End of Section 1 – Answers on pages 54–57]

[Now attempt the questions in Section 2]

Section 2

SECTION 2 – 70 marks

Attempt ALL questions.

MARKS

11 An app that contains a game has been created, and includes a high-score table stored in a separate sequential text file called scores.txt. Every time the game is played, the high-score table is shown and is updated and saved if appropriate at the end of every game.

   a) Using pseudocode, or a programming language with which you are familiar, complete the code below to read in ten names and high scores from the file into the arrays name and score:

   2

   Line 1   _____

   Line 2   FOR counter FROM 0 TO 9 DO

   Line 3   _____

   Line 4   _____

   Line 5   NEXT counter

   Line 6   _____

The game allows users to play with a group of three adventurers, each with a different name and a different rating for their strength, magic, speed and intelligence.

The game code features the record structure shown to allow this:

```
RECORD adventurer IS {STRING name, INTEGER strength,
INTEGER magic, INTEGER speed, INTEGER intelligence}
```

   b) The programmer wants to store the three adventurers' data using the record structure shown above. The array is to be named party.

   Using pseudocode, or a programming language of your choice, declare the array that can store the data for the three adventurers.

   2

   _____

   _____

The first character's details are shown below:

Name	Grek
Strength	19
Magic	3
Speed	6
Intelligence	4

c) Using pseudocode, or a programming language of your choice, write the code necessary to assign element zero of the array to the data for the adventurer shown in the table above.

Your answer should use the array declared in part (b).

3

The app allows users to interact over a chat feature. However, the creators have made use of censorship to block certain words or phrases from the chat.

d) Describe **one** possible concern that users may have over the censorship of the chat feature.

1

The app was tested on a mobile phone handset released two weeks ago, and performed as expected.

e) Describe **two** problems that may be encountered when testing the app on a handset released three years ago.

2

12 Kyle is using a database to keep track of music releases. The database has four linked tables:

Band	Band ID	PK
	Name	

Member	Member ID	PK
	Name	
	Band ID	FK

Album	Album ID	PK
	Name	
	Band ID	FK

Song	Song ID	PK
	Name	
	Album ID	FK
	Peak Chart Position	

a) Draw the entity relationship diagram showing the correct relationships between the four tables above.

3

Below is a partially complete data dictionary for the database:

Entity	Attribute	Key	Data type/size	Unique	Required	Validation
Band	Band ID	PK	Text (12)			
	Name		Text (50)			
Member	Member ID	PK	Text (8)		2	
	Name		Text (60)			
	Band ID	FK	Text (12)			
Album	Album ID	PK	Text (10)	1		
	Name		Text (100)			
	Band ID	FK	Text (12)			
Song	Song ID	PK	Text (10)			
	Name		Text (100)			
	Album ID	FK	Text (10)			3
	Peak Chart Position		Number			

b) Write what you would expect to be contained in the missing entries 1, 2 and 3.

2

1 _____

2 _____

3 _____

MARKS

Kyle has designed a form that opens when the database is loaded. The form includes buttons that allow a new record to be added to any of the tables.

c) Explain which type of user would benefit from the use of such a form and why they would find it useful.

1

_____

_____

d) Kyle would like a sound to be played each time the form loads. Explain how this could be achieved.

2

_____

_____

_____

13 Gillian has set up a website for a charity that employs staff to provide support to young carers. Young carers are young people who care for members of their family.

A friend has told Gillian that she should use meta tags to help with search engine optimisation. Gillian had been more concerned with optimising the load time of her web pages.

a) (i) Explain why Gillian should undertake search engine optimisation.

1

_____

_____

(ii) Where in the HTML code of a web page would you expect to find meta tags?

1

_____

(iii) Complete the following meta tag to include the terms 'young' and 'carers' as keywords for a web page:

1

```
<meta name = _____ content = _____>
```

Gillian includes a rule in the external stylesheet to make all the large headings appear in Garamond font wherever they appear on each page:

```
H1 {font-family:Garamond}
```

b) Rewrite the rule above so that in addition to those headings appearing in Garamond font (or similar), they are left-aligned wherever they appear on each page and also the text of the headings is red in colour.

2

_____

_____

The charity is concerned that they may not be fully complying with the Regulation of Investigatory Powers Act and asks Gillian for advice. The charity employs nine staff members who regularly communicate with one another and the young people via official charity email addresses.

c) Explain **two** responsibilities that the charity has under the Regulation of Investigatory Powers Act.

2

_____

_____

_____

_____

The charity is concerned at high utility bills caused by the heating system being switched on from early morning until late evening. This is because the various staff members and young people come and go from the offices at different times.

They are considering installing an intelligent heating system that will recognise trends in timings of office use, learn how quickly the office loses heat and access an online weather report to help adjust temperatures.

d) Explain **two** benefits of having such an intelligent heating system.

2

_____

_____

_____

_____

14 A client has asked CalumCorp to develop a program. Andy is part of a team developing a program using an Agile computing methodology.

a) Describe **one** advantage of this development methodology for the client.

1

_____

_____

b) When CalumCorp completes the program for the client, the client can decide whether to release it as open source or proprietary software.

Give **one** advantage of open source for the users of the software.

1

_____

_____

MARKS

c) CalumCorp will produce some documentation along with the software. Describe **two** items of documentation they might produce to issue to users.

2

_____

_____

_____

_____

d) Part of the program must include a section to find the total of any valid number in a list of three numbers. Valid numbers are 0 and above. An incomplete part of the test plan for this section is shown below:

	First number	Second number	Third number	Expected total	Actual total
Test 1	7	3	2	12	
Test 2	2	9	**X**		
Test 3	4	**Y**	5		

Write **two** different suitable values to be entered in place of the X and Y indicated in the table and explain your choice for each.

2

_____

_____

_____

_____

One programmer, Andy, has created this section in the program:

```
Line 1    SET numberArray TO [7,3,2]
Line 2    SET total TO 0
Line 3    FOR EACH number FROM numberArray DO
Line 4        IF number >= 0 THEN
Line 5            SET total TO total + number
Line 6        END IF
Line 7    END FOR
Line 8    SEND total TO DISPLAY
```

e) Andy now wants to store the highest valid number in a variable called `max`. He has to add four new lines in the spaces indicated in order to do this:

```
Line 1    SET numberArray TO [7,3,2]

Line 2    SET total TO 0

Line 3    _____

Line 4    FOR EACH number FROM numberArray DO

Line 5    IF number >= 0 THEN

Line 6        SET total TO total + number

Line 7        _____

Line 8        _____

Line 9        _____

Line 10   END IF

Line 11   END FOR

Line 12   SEND total TO DISPLAY
```

Write the four missing lines of code.

2

15 Sophia has created a website for a wedding planning business. She has some photographs on a memory card. The card is inserted into a card reader on her laptop, and she intends to upload these photographs to the website.

a) Describe **two** functions of the operating system and explain how each will be involved in the transfer of the photographs from the memory card onto the hard drive of Sophia's laptop.

4

_____

_____

_____

_____

_____

_____

b) The photographs are stored as bitmap file types rather than using vector storage. Explain why vector storage is not suitable for photographs.

1

_____

_____

_____

c) Sophia has uploaded a vector graphic to the website. It is a diagram of one wedding venue layout that she has found to be popular:

Describe **two** advantages of vector storage over bitmap storage for an image like the one shown.

2

_____

_____

_____

_____

16 Roberta regularly gets clothing and badges from an online shop called 'Style Printing'.

a) Identify **one** area of the web page that requires a client-side script to be executed.

1

_____

b) Identify **one** area of the web page that requires a server-side script to be executed.

1

_____

c) When Roberta uses the same browser on the same device to access other websites, she sees adverts for the Style Printing site appearing on those web pages. Explain why those websites have specifically shown adverts for Style Printing to Roberta.

2

_____

_____

_____

_____

d) Roberta's friend Graham is using his laptop to access the Style Printing site. However, Graham has problems with his vision, and is finding the text on the site difficult to read. How could Style Printing ensure that vision impairment does not prevent users from being able to read text on the site?

1

_____

_____

e) The Style Print website uses asymmetric encryption to ensure that payment data is secure through the use of a public key and a private key. Explain the steps involved in Style Print securely receiving data from a user using this.

17 Malala is using a desktop computer to develop a new app for mobile devices. She is using the rapid application development design methodology.

a) Describe **two** benefits to a client of Malala following a rapid application development methodology.

2

Malala could code the app in either a high level language or a low level language. Malala is concerned that a low level language is not very similar to English.

b) Explain **one** other reason why a low level language would not be suitable in this scenario.

2

Malala wishes to use her desktop computer to see how the app would perform on a smartphone.

c) Explain how it is possible to run an app for a smartphone on a desktop computer.

2

Rehman has told Malala that it is easier to code the program using global variables. However, she makes use of parameter passing instead.

d) **(i)** Describe **two** risks that Rehman takes in always using global variables in his code.

2

_____

_____

_____

_____

(ii) Malala has passed some arrays as parameters into the procedures. Explain the benefits of passing arrays by reference instead of by value.

2

_____

_____

_____

e) Malala has used some procedures and some functions. Explain how procedures are different from functions.

2

_____

_____

_____

18 Bernard is designing a new embedded computer system to run inside a new model of petrol-powered car that is being developed. The system will take input from multiple sensors as well as from user actions and be responsible for a number of functions including climate control, antilock braking system, fuel injection, satellite navigation and in-car audio.

a) Explain how Bernard could ensure the new system has the hardware required to carry out the multiprogramming required in this situation.

2

_____

_____

_____

MARKS

b) Describe **two** possible environmental implications of Bernard's embedded computer system.

2

_____

_____

_____

_____

c) Bernard has designed a microprocessor that fetches instructions from main memory and executes them in sequence. Describe the steps involved in the fetch–execute cycle.

3

_____

_____

_____

_____

_____

d) The car manufacturer decides to carry out usability testing on the whole system. Explain how the manufacturers can try to ensure the whole system is tested during this.

2

_____

_____

_____

[End of Section 2 – Answers on pages 58–67]
[END OF PRACTICE PAPER A]

Higher Computing Science

B

Duration – 2 hours

Total marks – 90

SECTION 1 – 20 marks

Attempt ALL questions.

SECTION 2 – 70 marks

Attempt ALL questions.

Show all workings.

In the exam you must write your answers in the answer booklet provided and clearly identify the question number you are attempting.

Use **blue or black** ink.

Section 1

MARKS

1   Two's complement can be used to represent both positive and negative numbers. State the highest positive number and the lowest negative number that can be represented using 12-bit two's complement representation.

2

2   Gerry's program has just reached the testing stage of the software development process. Explain why the software development process could be said to be an iterative process.

2

3   A stereo sound file lasting one minute with a sample rate of 48 kHz and a file size of 11 250 Kb is stored on a computer.

Calculate the sample depth of the audio file. Show all working and express your answer in appropriate units.

3

MARKS

4 One method for improving system performance is the use of cache memory. Explain how the use of cache would speed up the execution of the following code, which calculates the volume of a room:

```
SET roof_height TO peak_height - wall_height
SET lower_volume TO wall_height × length × width
SET upper_volume TO (roof_height × length × width)/3
SET room_volume TO lower_volume + upper_volume
```

2

_____

_____

_____

_____

_____

5 Describe **one** cost to a company that has been affected by a denial of service attack.

1

_____

_____

6 Electronic communications are often kept secure during transmission through use of public and private keys.

a) Explain the purpose of the public key in this situation.

1

_____

_____

b) Explain why having access to a company's public key does not help criminals to access encrypted communications from customers to the company.

1

_____

_____

7 There are many disabilities or impairments that can be a barrier to effective computer use.

State an item of hardware and describe how it could be used to aid those with motor or dexterity impairment.

1

_____

_____

MARKS

8 Describe the features of a declarative language used in the creation of software.

2

_____

_____

_____

_____

9 A radio station is creating a program to store details about songs. The details stored are: track name, artist name and highest chart position.

a) Show how a record structure would be created to store the necessary song details.

2

_____

_____

b) Create a data structure using your record structure from part (a) that can store the data for 5000 songs.

2

_____

_____

10 Tiana has written a program that involves storing text files. Give **one** reason why the use of ASCII might be preferable to Unicode for storage of text.

1

_____

_____

[End of Section 1 – Answers on pages 68–70]

[Now attempt the questions in Section 2]

Section 2

MARKS

11 Fleur is a company that makes and sells packs of tea bags for various flavours of tea. They have a desktop application that allows them to keep track of their sales.

For each type of tea, the number of packs sold that week is stored in an array called `sold`, and the name of the type of tea is stored in an array called `name`:

name	jasmine	cinnamon	camomile	dusk	pink	autumn	green	detox
sold	18	16	15	16	65	65	30	3

a) The sales statistics feature allows the user to enter a type of tea, and displays a message:

`The number of sales of dusk was 16`

(i) Write, using pseudocode or a language with which you are familiar, an algorithm that can:

- find the number of sales for the type of tea entered by the user
- display a similar message to that shown above, or an error message if that type is not in the list.

The type of tea entered by the user will be held in a variable called `target_name`.

7

(ii) The manager wishes a feature in the program to state how many types of tea sold 30 or more packs in one month. Complete the following code to implement this feature:

Line 1   `SET total TO 0`

Line 2   `FOR index FROM 0 TO 7 DO`

Line 3   _____

Line 4   _____

Line 5   _____

Line 6   `END FOR`

Line 7   `SEND total & "types of tea sold 30 or more packs this month" TO DISPLAY`

2

b) To access the sales-statistics feature, the user must click the appropriate icon within the desktop application's window.

(i) Explain what the Memory Management function of the operating system will do when the user clicks the icon to load the sales-statistics feature.

1

_____

(ii) Explain what the file management function of the operating system will do when the file 'result.txt' is to be saved to the hard drive.

1

_____

_____

c) The following code is used with the `sold` array as shown above to calculate the overall power used per day:

```
DECLARE total AS INTEGER INITIALLY 0
FOR product FROM 0 TO 7 DO
    SET total TO total + sold(product)
    SEND total TO DISPLAY
NEXT product
```

Part of a trace table is shown below. Entries (i) and (ii) are missing. What should be entered in those spaces?

2

Product	0	1	2	3
Sold	18	16	15	16
Total	18	34	(i)	(ii)

(i) _____

(ii) _____

d) Fleur has decided to stop selling the 'detox' type of tea due to poor sales, and the array now contains this data for the following month:

name	jasmine	cinnamon	camomile	dusk	pink	autumn	green
sold	19	26	14	19	60	47	39

However, this change results in an error when the programmer runs the code from part (c).

Explain why the error occurs and what change could be made to the code from part (c) to correct the error.

2

_____

_____

_____

_____

e) Fleur also has an app that is installed on the manager's smartphone, which works together with energy-monitoring software on the desktop computer in the office. The company has designed an intelligent system that can make use of the data collected from both the smartphone and the desktop to reduce the power usage of the desktop.

Suggest **one** way in which such an intelligent system could reduce power usage by a desktop computer.

2

_____

_____

_____

12 Dani runs a shop in Canada that sells goods such as toiletries, drinks and snacks imported from Scotland. She decides to keep track of this information in a database with four tables:

Product	Product ID	PK
	Name	
	Description	
	Category	FK
	Manufacturer	FK

Category	Name	PK
	Description	
	Current discount	

Exporter	Exporter ID	PK
	Name	
	Address	
	Tel no.	

Manufacturer	Manufacturer ID	PK
	Name	
	Address	
	Tel no.	
	Exporter	

a) Show the correct entity-relationship diagram to indicate the relationship between the four tables above.

3

Dani's customers can browse her database from a kiosk within the shop. After a customer submits a query, the screen below is shown:

b) **(i)** State the tables and fields used to show the screen pictured above.

3

_____

_____

_____

_____

_____

(ii) State the criteria used in the search query above.

1

_____

Dani is updating the website for her business. She has included the ability to query the database from the website, and the results show in a black and white layout similar to that pictured above.

c) Dani wishes to make the text 'Dani International' stand out in blue whenever the user moves the pointer onto those words.

In the body section, Dani has placed the following:

```
<h1 id = "dani" onmouseover = "mouseOver()" Dani
International</h1>
```

Write the text needed below this in the body section to cause the heading 'Dani International' to stand out in blue whenever the user moves the pointer over those words.

4

d) Dani wishes to use a meta tag so that if users use a search engine to search for 'Scottish' or 'Canada', her website is more likely to appear further up the list of search results.

Complete the following: 2

```
<meta name = _____ content = _____ >
```

e) Dani makes use of cloud-based services for data storage. Describe another cloud-based service and how it could benefit Dani.

2

13 Bereket's program is used to calculate charges for hiring bicycles. The departure and return times are converted to and stored as real numbers, for example 08:30 hours will be converted to and stored as 8.5.

The function below is used to calculate the cost of hire for each bike.

```
Line 1    FUNCTION calcCost(REAL departure, REAL return)
          RETURNS REAL
Line 2        DECLARE hours_hired INITIALLY 0
Line 3        DECLARE total_charge INITIALLY 0
Line 4        SET hours_hired TO return-departure
Line 5        IF hours_hired <= 1 THEN
Line 6           SET total_charge TO 5
Line 7           IF hours_hired <= 2 THEN
Line 8              SET total_charge TO 8
Line 9           ELSE
Line 10             SET total_charge TO 12.5
Line 11          END IF
Line 12       END IF
Line 13   RETURN total_charge
Line 14   END FUNCTION
```

This function is called using the line below:

```
SET cost TO calcCost(left, back)
```

a) Name an **actual** parameter from the code above, and describe what is meant by an actual parameter.

2

_____

_____

_____

b) Elena notices errors when testing Bereket's program. If the bike has been hired for more than one hour but less than or equal to two, the cost wrongly shows as zero.

(i) What cost will show if the bike was hired at 10:00 and returned at 10:30?

1

_____

(ii) State how to change the code above to remove the errors.

1

_____

c) Elena made use of a breakpoint while testing the program. Explain how a breakpoint is used.

2

_____

_____

_____

d) Identify how the parameter 'left' would be passed into the function, and explain the reason for your answer.

2

_____

_____

e) The calling program contains a variable called `hours_hired`. Explain why this variable is unaffected by the `hours_hired` variable contained within the calcCost function above.

1

_____

14 Alford Kits sell sporting equipment through a database-driven website. One page generated by the website and displayed on a client's browser is shown below:

a) Describe the benefits of using usability testing on the website above.

2

_____

_____

_____

_____

MARKS

b) Identify **one** part of the web page that has made use of client-side scripting.

1

_____

c) Explain how the use of a database-driven website would allow the Alford Kits website to display the search results shown above.

2

_____

_____

_____

_____

d) Alford Kits performs a full backup of all their data once a week.

(i) Explain why this backup schedule is not sufficient.

1

_____

_____

(ii) Describe another backup schedule that should also be used in this case.

3

_____

_____

e) Alford Kits makes use of a hybrid cloud to store a backup of all their web pages and the designs for new kits to be released next year.
Explain how a hybrid cloud is different from a public cloud.

2

_____

_____

_____

_____

f) Two ideas for Alford Kits' latest cricket bat design are shown below:

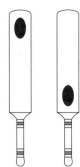

The two designs are identical apart from the position of the black oval.

(i) Explain how the first design would be changed to the second design using a bit-mapped graphics package.

1

_____

_____

(ii) Explain how the first design would be changed to the second design using a vector graphics package.

1

_____

_____

g) The original cricket bat design currently on sale looks like this:

(i) Explain the difference, if any, in file size from this design to the new designs shown above in part (f) if the files were all saved as vector graphics.

2

_____

_____

_____

(ii) Explain the difference, if any, in file size from this design to the new designs shown above in part (f) if the files were all saved as bitmapped graphics.

2

_____

_____

_____

15 Boris runs his own business recording footage of weddings and uses a computer system to edit the videos.

a) Boris has created a poster to advertise his business. The poster is saved as a bitmapped image file and is compressed using DCT compression and then RLE compression.

   (i) Explain how RLE compresses bitmapped graphics.

2

_____

_____

_____

   (ii) Explain how the use of DCT increases the effectiveness of RLE compression.

2

_____

_____

_____

b) Boris has recorded part of a wedding video where the groom is standing in one place giving a speech. He has also recorded another part of the wedding where there are a number of couples dancing.

He has compressed the videos using both interframe and intraframe compression.

   (i) Boris notices that before compression the two videos took up approximately the same amount of storage space. However, following compression, the compressed version of the second video featuring dancing takes up a lot more storage space than the compressed version of the first video featuring the speech. Explain why this is the case.

2

_____

_____

_____

_____

   (ii) The hardware Boris is using for playback has sufficient capabilities that he has been able to view many high-quality videos with no problems. Despite this, when he plays both the compressed and uncompressed versions of the videos described he notices that the movement looks jerky and unrealistic. Explain why this might be the case.

1

_____

_____

c) Boris has set up a website for his business. The code from part of one page for the site is shown below:

```
<!DOCTYPE html>
<html>
   <head>
      <style>
         p{color:green; text-align: center}
      </style>
   </head>
   <body>
      <p> Welcome To </p>
      <p style = "color:blue; font-size:200%;"< Boris
      Romanov</p>
      <p> Videography </p>
   </body>
</html>
```

Describe the output from this code.

3

_____

_____

_____

_____

_____

d) Boris has chosen to use proprietary software to edit his videos. Explain what is meant by proprietary software and give **one** advantage to Boris of using this type of software.

2

_____

_____

_____

_____

[End of Section 2 – Answers on pages 71–79]

[END OF PRACTICE PAPER B]

Higher Computing Science

C

Duration – 2 hours

Total marks – 90

SECTION 1 – 20 marks

Attempt ALL questions.

SECTION 2 – 70 marks

Attempt ALL questions.

Show all workings.

In the exam you must write your answers in the answer booklet provided and clearly identify the question number you are attempting.

Use **blue** or **black** ink.

Section 1

SECTION 1 – 20 marks

Attempt ALL questions.

MARKS

1 Convert the 8-bit two's complement number 1000 1100 into denary. 1

2 Part of a program that calculates total annual rainfall is shown below. The code makes use of a function to add up a total of four numbers:

Line 1 `GET autumn FROM keyboard`

Line 2 `GET winter FROM keyboard`

Line 3 `GET spring FROM keyboard`

Line 4 `GET summer FROM keyboard`

Line 5 `SET total_rainfall TO total(autumn, winter,`
`spring, summer)`

Identify **one** argument from the code above and explain what is meant by an argument. 2

3 A real number is stored using 32-bit floating point representation. The mantissa is allocated 8 bits, and 24 bits are allocated to the exponent. Describe the effect if the allocation is changed to a 16-bit mantissa and a 16-bit exponent. 2

4 Procedural languages are often used to create programs to solve problems. Describe **two** features of procedural languages. 2

5 Lesley's Toy Shop has recently created a new computer game and ensured that this program is portable. Give **one** economic benefit to Lesley of the game being portable.

_____

_____

1

6 Below is part of a program that checks that the correct password has been entered before showing an account balance.

Line 1   REPEAT

Line 2   GET password FROM keyboard

Line 3   UNTIL password = correct_password

Line 4   SEND balance TO DISPLAY

Explain the impact of cache on the execution of instructions 3 and 4.

_____

_____

_____

_____

2

7 Ruth is developing a new social media platform for fans of animated film and television. Describe the safeguards required to ensure users' privacy on social media sites.

_____

_____

_____

_____

2

8 Stephanie has created an external CSS stylesheet called `webstyle`. Complete the HTML code that will successfully link to this stylesheet.

2

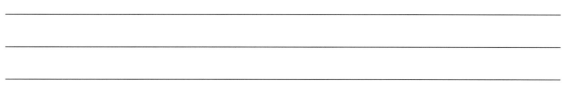

```
<_____ rel = "stylesheet" _____ = "text/css"
href = "webstyle.css">
```

9 There are many disabilities or impairments that can be a barrier to effective computer use.

a) Holly has a visual impairment. One way this could be overcome is by using high-contrast colour schemes. State **one** other feature that could help Holly.

_____

_____

1

b) Arnold has a hearing impairment. One way this could be overcome is by adjusting the speaker volume. State **one** other feature that could help Arnold.

1

_____

_____

10 The home page on Montford Zoo's website has some dynamic content that automatically links to a weather website and shows the weather forecast for the day. The zoo management is concerned that users who notice bad weather on a particular day may decide not to visit. Give **two** other disadvantages of having this dynamic feature on the web page.

2

_____

_____

_____

_____

11 Hector has been editing some graphics, and has now compressed the graphics using LZW encoding.
Explain how LZW encoding compresses data.

2

_____

_____

_____

_____

[End of Section 1 – Answers on pages 80–83]

[Now attempt the questions in Section 2]

C

Section 2

MARKS

12 Jiong is creating a program to process weather statistics for each of Scotland's 32 local authorities.

He has decided that using a record structure is the best way to do this. He has added the following record structure:

```
RECORD council IS {STRING name, REAL annual_rainfall,
INTEGER hours_sunshine, REAL average_windspeed}
```

He went on to declare an array of records using:

```
DECLARE authority(32) AS council
```

a) Jiong wishes to read in the data for the 32 entries from a text file called stats.txt. Show, using pseudocode or a programming language that you are familiar with, how he would do this.

4

b) Renewable energy can be produced by wind turbines. Jiong wishes to use the data he has within the program to determine the name of the local authority that has the highest windspeed. His friend Rebekah has written the following function, which she suggests he use within his program:

```
FUNCTION findHighest (ARRAY OF INTEGER list) RETURNS INTEGER
DECLARE highest AS INTEGER INITIALLY list(0)
FOR index FROM 1 TO 31 DO
   IF list(index)>highest THEN
     SET highest TO list(index)
   END IF
END FOR
RETURN highest
END FUNCTION
```

Suggest **two** reasons why Jiong cannot use the function as it is shown above to find the name of the local authority with the highest average windspeed.

2

_____

_____

_____

_____

13 Clarissa works for Dunton Juniors football club. She is writing a program to analyse data held on season-ticket holders at the club.

The program includes an array of integers called age to hold the age that each season-ticket holder was when they bought their current season ticket. Clarissa wants a program to use this array to show on screen how many season-ticket holders are under the age of 18. There are 300 season-ticket holders this season.

a) Show, using pseudocode or a programming language that you are familiar with, how she would do this.

5

b) Customers pay for their tickets on the Dunton Juniors website. However, because this is a small local business, some customers are concerned when they log on to the site that they are not on the genuine Dunton Juniors website. Explain how Dunton Juniors could reassure those customers.

2

_____

_____

_____

_____

c) Customers log in using an eight-digit ID number then a four-digit PIN.

Some customers are concerned that their login data could be captured by keylogger programs.

Describe **one** way that Dunton Juniors could help prevent sensitive data being captured by keylogger programs on client computers during the login process.

1

_____

_____

d) Clarissa is concerned that customers who enter relevant keywords into a search engine are still finding that they have to click through two pages of results to find the club's web page. Suggest what changes could be made to ensure the site is ranked more highly by search engines.

2

_____

_____

_____

_____

e) The club stores a lot of data on its network, including players' medical information; season-ticket holders' contact and payment details; notes from the coaches and manager about players; and tactics and sales data.

The club wishes only medical personnel to access the medical information, only office staff to access the customer information and only coaching staff to access the tactical information.

Explain how the club's network could be set up to ensure that only appropriate groups of staff can access the data relevant to their role.

2

_____

_____

f) The coaching team wants Clarissa to move certain information to offline storage. Explain **one** advantage of storing data in offline storage.

1

_____

_____

g) Some matchday photos have been taken on a digital camera. When the photos are taken, they are automatically compressed using DCT. Back at the club office, the camera is connected to a computer in order to transfer the photos.

(i) Describe **one** disadvantage of compressing the photos using DCT.

1

_____

_____

(ii) Explain why the interface will not perform analogue-to-digital conversion when handling transfer of the photos between the camera and the computer.

1

_____

_____

_____

_____

(iii) State **two** functions of the operating system involved and describe their role when transferring these photographs to the computer.

4

_____

_____

_____

_____

_____

h) Some interviews with club personnel have been made available on the website as audio files.

They have first been compressed using Free Lossless Audio Codec. Explain how Free Lossless Audio Codec would compress this data.

2

_____

_____

_____

_____

14 Paterson Dirt Moto is a business that allows customers to take motorised dirt-bike lessons at various locations around the UK. Each location features a number of dirt bike tracks and trails, varying in difficulty.

A database has been set up to keep track of the relevant information.

Resort	Name	
	Description	
	Address	
	Resort Postcode	PK
	Tel No.	

Track	Track Name	PK
	Description	
	Difficulty	
	Resort Postcode	FK
	Image	

Booking	Booking ID	PK
	Resort Postcode	FK
	Date	
	Time	
	No. Riders	
	Customer Name	

Instructor	Instructor ID	PK
	Name	
	Address	
	Tel No.	
	Resort Postcode	FK

a) Identify **one** field from above that is a surrogate key.

1

b) Draw the entity relationship diagram for the database shown above.

3

c) Paterson Dirt Moto wishes to store whether each booking has been paid or not. Describe what change would be made to the database to allow this.

_____

d) Paterson Dirt Moto wishes to allow customers to use a computer terminal in the reception office at each resort, so that customers can search for tracks by difficulty or resort name. Describe how this could be done using features of database software.

_____

_____

_____

_____

_____

_____

e) The company makes use of distributed storage across their different UK resorts to store the database.

(i) Describe **two** advantages to Paterson Dirt Moto of this method of database storage.

_____

_____

_____

(ii) Suggest **one** concern that office workers may have over this method of database storage.

_____

_____

(iii) Suggest a transmission medium that would be used for access to the distributed storage.

_____

f) Paterson Dirt Moto plans to release an app that allows people to use a simulation of some real tracks and control a virtual bike around the tracks, in the hope that this will draw in some more business.

Describe how Paterson Dirt Moto could ensure that all customers could use the software regardless of the operating system on their device.

2

_____

_____

_____

_____

g) Each bike contains a GPS transponder that continually updates the office on the position of the bike as it travels around the track.

(i) Explain **two** ways in which an intelligent system could use this data to ensure the safety of customers.

2

_____

_____

_____

_____

(ii) Explain how the use of a multicore processor could aid in processing the GPS data.

2

_____

_____

_____

_____

15 Callum is writing a program to keep track of pupil scores in a primary school maths challenge. He has decided to use a high level language to create the program.

a) Describe **two** features of a high level language.

2

_____

_____

_____

_____

b) When data for the score is input into the program, it is validated as it must be a whole number in the range 0 to 100 inclusive. Create a test plan to check the effectiveness of the validation.

3

_____

_____

_____

_____

_____

_____

c) A separate part of the program is going to be tested with the following two arrays, one array containing eight names and one array containing eight scores:

Name	Amy	Brian	Cerys	Daniel	Erica	Filip	Gillian	Harry
Score	18	0	100	1	99	100	65	32

Callum is to make this part of the program show the name of any pupil who gained a score of 100. Using pseudocode, or a language with which you are familiar, show how this could be done.

3

d) The primary school's logo is stored as a bit-mapped graphic rather than a vector graphic. Give **one** advantage of storing the logo as a bit-mapped graphic.

1

_____

16 Candice is developing a new mobile smartphone for Iodyne Technologies. The smartphone includes a camera for capturing still images and video.

a) Characteristics of stored video include resolution, bit depth and frame rate. Explain the term 'frame rate' with respect to video.

1

_____

_____

b) The video capture and editing app has a screen that shows a large preview of the video with an area at the bottom to add a comment and three graphical buttons that allow a user to share the clip to social media, exit the app or view a menu. Clicking the video preview square will play the video full screen with sound.

Draw a fully labelled wireframe of the user interface for this screen.

3

c) One fairly large program for use on the smartphone is going to be developed using the step-wise refinement methodology.

(i) Explain the approach taken to designing a solution using step-wise refinement.

2

_____

_____

_____

(ii) Give **one** advantage of how the step-wise refinement methodology could reduce development time in this situation.

1

_____

_____

d) Programmers often use watchpoints during the testing stage. Explain what is meant by a watchpoint and how it is used at the testing stage.

2

_____

_____

_____

_____

e) Some of the apps are tested using beta testing. Give **two** advantages of making use of beta testing in this situation.

2

_____

_____

_____

_____

f) After the phone and a few apps have been released, one of the apps requires an update to be downloaded. Give **two** reasons why the app may have had an update released.

2

_____

_____

_____

_____

g) One user has an earlier smartphone released by Iodyne Technologies. They have successfully downloaded to their phone one of the apps for the new Iodyne Technologies smartphone. Explain **one** issue the user may encounter when they try to run the app.

1

_____

_____

h) Explain **one** possible environmental impact of Iodyne Technologies deciding to release this new smartphone.

1

_____

_____

_____

[End of Section 2 – Answers on pages 84–93]

[END OF PRACTICE PAPER C]

Higher
Computing
Science

Practice Paper A

Section 1

(Where appropriate, hints contain the page number of the relevant corresponding material from *How To Pass Higher Computing Science* by Greg Reid, published by Hodder Gibson. See www.hoddereducation.co.uk for details.)

Question	Answer	Hint
1	10100100 (1 mark)	Positive 92 would be 01011100 Invert the bits to get 10100011 Add one to get 10100100 You can always convert it back again to check your answer. *(For an alternative method, see HTP pp.22–23.)*
2	Unicode can represent a greater range of characters than ASCII. (1 mark)	Unicode uses 16 bits per character so can store 2^{16} (65 536) characters. ASCII only uses 7 bits per character. Answers referring to Unicode being able to represent non-English language characters must still refer to the greater range of characters that can be represented by Unicode. With ASCII, the 8th bit is used as a check digit to take it up to 8 bits. *(HTP p.23)*
3	$11 \times 30 \times 1920 \times 1080 \times 8$ $= 5\,474\,304\,000$ bits $= 684\,288\,000$ bytes $= 668\,250$ kilobytes $= 652.59$ megabytes (rounded to 2 decimal places) (1 mark for correct multiplication sum) (1 mark for correct conversion of units)	File size in bits = duration in seconds multiplied by frame rate in frames per second multiplied by resolution of one frame multiplied by bit depth in bits. To convert bits to bytes, divide by 8. To convert bytes to kilobytes, or to convert kilobytes to megabytes, divide by 1024. SQA will accept rounding of the final answer to the nearest whole number or to a reasonable number of decimal places, if the answer is rounded correctly. *(HTP p.27)*

Question			Answer	Hint
4			The subclass will inherit the methods/attributes of the parent class. (1 mark) Lesley need only define the additional attributes/methods required. (1 mark)	The subclass will take on the attributes (variables) of the parent class and the methods of the parent class. The programmer would still have to define additional attributes and methods for the subclass – it wouldn't stay identical to the parent class or else there would be no point in creating the subclass. *(HTP pp.3–4)*
5			Any two of: ■ Inspect the documentation on the system currently in use ■ Observe the system currently in use ■ Create a prototype of the solution and ask for feedback from the client (2 marks)	One answer that appears in some textbooks but does not appear in SQA marking guidelines is the issuing of questionnaires, so avoid this answer. The analysis stage is the initial stage in the software development process. Creating the software specification correctly at this early stage will help programmers to be sure that their solution is correct as it is developed at the design and implementation stages. Part of this may involve looking at the current system already in use. The software specification will form the basis of a legal contract between the client and the programming company; this is another reason why its accuracy is important. *(HTP p.17)*
6	a)		A hub transmits data packets to all stations on the network. (1 mark)	The hub does not look at the address of the intended destination of a data packet, but will instead copy the packet and send it down all the channels of the network. A channel can then be carrying data packets that are not for any devices connected to that channel.
	b)		A switch only sends data packets to the device they are meant for. (1 mark) This improves network performance due to fewer collisions. (1 mark)	Each data packet will have a header that contains information about the data packet. The header will include the address of the device that is the packet's intended destination. The switch will look at that address and send the packet along the correct channel. The other channels are then not carrying the packet unnecessarily.

Question			Answer	Hint
7	a)		Data is lost during compression. (1 mark)	Compression involves storing the data in a different way so that it takes up less storage capacity, and takes less time to transmit. Lossy compression will involve getting rid of some of the data while still trying to keep as high quality as possible. Lossless compression will involve storing the data in a different way that keeps all of the original data and quality. Run length encoding (RLE) is an example of lossless compression, whereas discrete cosine transform (DCT) is an example of lossy compression. *(HTP p.56)*
	b)		Removes sounds that humans cannot hear OR Removes the quieter of two similar sounds (1 mark)	Some frequencies that are not in the range that humans can hear are still picked up by recording equipment and stored. Perceptual coding will remove this data. Where two similar sounds are present, the quieter one will be removed, as this would most likely be drowned out by the louder one when the sound is played. *(HTP pp.57–58)*
8			`IF parcel_code(iteration) = target_code THEN` OR `IF target_code = parcel_code(iteration) THEN` (1 mark)	This is an example of the linear search algorithm. The loop exits if it has checked all the 18 parcels. The missing line is needed to set the Boolean variable 'found' to true if the correct parcel is found. This variable was set to false before the loop was started. Remember arrays are indexed from zero. *(HTP p.10)*
9	a)		A compound key is two or more fields combined so as to uniquely identify each record in a database. (1 mark) In this example, there could be a problem if two staff members have the same forename, surname and designation. (1 mark)	For the first mark, you must express both the fact that multiple fields are used together and that this is to ensure you can have a unique reference for each record in the database. *(HTP p.41)*
	b)		Any one of: ■ Add a new field and use `"Autonumber"` to decide the contents ■ Add a new field and decide an arbitrary number/text ID for each record (1 mark)	A surrogate key is an extra field added to the database to uniquely identify each record in a database. The field added is not a required piece of data about the staff member, but is instead extra artificial (made-up) data only so they can have a unique ID. The `"Autonumber"` field type is often used for this in popular database applications. Your SQA candidate number is an example of a surrogate key.

Question			Answer	Hint
10	**a)**		Any one of: ■ If a hacker were to gain access to the network, they cannot access data in offline storage ■ If a virus were to infect the network, it cannot corrupt data in offline storage ■ Physical methods of preventing access to the storage media can be used (1 mark)	Offline storage is when files are stored on backing storage that is not connected to the network. Usually this involves a computer in a locked room for access to this data. Other security measures can be put in place for access to that room, e.g. biometrics such as fingerprint scanners.
	b)		*Advantage:* Any one of: ■ Maintenance will be carried out by the company providing the cloud service ■ Security will be implemented by the company providing the cloud service ■ Backup will be implemented by the company providing the cloud service (1 mark) *Disadvantage:* Any one of: ■ A connection is required to be able to access the data and this connection could go down ■ Patients may not be happy that their sensitive data is being stored by a third party as they may fear others accessing it, e.g. hackers or cloud service employees (1 mark)	Often SQA will accept a number of valid answers. However, the key is to give detail, show technical knowledge and refer to the situation. *(HTP p.67)*

Section 2

Question			Answer	Hint

11	a)		```OPEN FILE "scores.txt"```
			```FOR counter FROM 0 TO 9 DO```
			```RECEIVE name(counter) FROM```
			```FILE```
			```RECEIVE score(counter) FROM```
			```FILE```
			```NEXT counter```
			```CLOSE FILE```
			(1 mark for correct open and close lines)
			(1 mark for two correct lines to read contents into array)
				The file operations that you may be asked to use are listed by SQA in the Course Assessment Specification: CREATE, OPEN, READ, WRITE, CLOSE. Be sure to use the filename and array/variable names given in the question.
				(HTP p.7)

	b)		```DECLARE party[2] As```
			```adventurer```
			(2 marks)
				A record allows a set of variables, with different types, to be named and organised under one data structure. DIM in place of DECLARE would also be acceptable. Be sure to use the array name party as this is given in the question. The [2] indicates the array size – this will set up an array of three adventurer records called party[0], party[1] and party[2].
				(HTP p.7)

	c)		```SET party[0].name TO "Grek"```
			```SET party[0].strength TO 19```
			```SET party[0].magic TO 3```
			```SET party[0].speed TO 6```
			```SET party[0].intelligence```
			```TO 4```
			OR
			```DECLARE party[0] INITIALLY```
			```adventurer ("Grek", 19, 3,```
			```6, 4)```
			OR
			```SET party[0] TO adventurer```
			```("Grek", 19, 3, 6, 4)```
			(1 mark for use of array declared in part (b), e.g.
			party[ ].)
			(1 mark for use of dot to indicate correct field names)
			(1 mark for correct entries into fields)
				The order you will often see is a line to define the record (in this case this is given in the question), then a line to create an instance of that record – usually as an array (this is the answer to part (b)), then code to assign values to the attributes/fields within an instance of the record (the answer shown here in part (c)).
				(HTP p.7)

Question			Answer	Hint
	d)		Users may feel that this limits freedom of speech. (1 mark)	While you may be tempted to give other relevant answers, this is the answer taken from the Course Assessment Specification, and so is sure to be accepted by markers. *(HTP p.76)*
	e)		Any two of: ■ There may not be enough storage space to install the app ■ There may not be enough main memory to run the app ■ The processor may not be fast enough to run the app ■ The handset may not be able to run the version of the operating system needed to run the app (2 marks)	An older handset will tend only to be able to update up to a certain version of the operating system. It will also tend to have poorer specification in both processor and storage. *(HTP p.62)*
12	**a)**		Member Band Album Song (3 marks)	For two tables to have a relationship, one of the tables must contain a field that is a foreign key, i.e. the primary key from the other table. Whichever table contains the foreign key is on the 'many' side of a relationship with the table for which that field is the primary key. The answer given here is to the standard required by SQA. *(However, a more detailed version is found on HTP pp.40–41)*
	b)		1 Y 2 Y (1 mark) 3 Lookup from Album table (1 mark)	1 The field indicated is the primary key for the Member table; there must be an entry in this field for every record in that table so that each different member can be uniquely identified. 2 The field indicated is the primary key for the Album table; the entry in this field must be unique for every record in that table so that each different album can be uniquely identified. 3 There can be no entries in this field in the song table of albums that don't exist in the album table. A song must appear on an existing album in this database example. *(HTP p.42)*
	c)		Any one of: ■ Novices/beginners because it makes it easy for them to operate the database ■ Novices/beginners because no expert knowledge is required to perform tasks on the database (1 mark)	The two user types are novices and experts. Novices require a user-friendly interface as they will have little or no technical knowledge.

Question			Answer	Hint
	d)		Edit the scripting language within the database software (1 mark) for the form open/load event. (1 mark)	Scripting languages within general purpose packages such as database software allow functionality to be added that was not originally part of the package. There will be existing scripts for events that can occur within the package that code can be added to.
13	**a)**	**(i)**	Any one of: ■ To get more hits by making her page more easily found by search engines ■ To get more hits by getting her page ranked more highly by search engines (1 mark)	There are a number of techniques that will improve how highly a search engine ranks a page. They include having a relevant URL, an appropriate title tag, meta tags with appropriate keywords, ensuring there are more links to the site from other sites, submitting the website to search engines and keyword loading/stuffing (adding more relevant text content to the body of the web pages).
		(ii)	Any one of: ■ Between the `<HEAD>` and `</HEAD>` tags ■ In the head section (1 mark)	The head section will contain title and meta HTML tags, then the body section will contain the text that actually appears on the web page and also include HTML tags for formatting, hyperlinks, images, etc. *(HTP p.49)*

		(iii)	`<meta name = "keywords" content = "young, carers">`
			(1 mark)
				The quotation marks are required.
				The structure of a meta tag is to include attributes within the tag, e.g:
				`<meta name = "keywords" content = "Hodder, Gibson, Computing, revision">`
				`<meta name = "author" content = "David Alford">`
				`<meta name = "description" content = "Higher Computing Science revision resources from Hodder Gibson">`
				`<meta charset = "UTF-8">`
				(HTP p.49)

	b)		`H2 {font-family:Garamond; text-align:left; color:red}`
			OR
			`H2 {font-family:Garamond; text-align:left; color: rgb(255, 0, 0)}`
			OR
			`H2 {font-family:Garamond; text-align:left; color: #ff0000}`
			(2 marks)
				The first answer given is the expected one, but the others are also correct. Be sure to use the American spelling of 'color'. The order of the three declarations is not important; it could equally be `H2 {text-align:left; color:red; font-family:Garamond}`
				(HTP pp.50, 82–83)

Question			Answer	Hint
	c)		Any two of: - Inform employees that authorities may have access to digital communication - Provide access/encryption keys to authorised authorities - Have facilities to store digital communications - Have facilities to monitor digital communications (2 marks)	The Regulation of Investigatory Powers Act applies only to digital communications, so be sure to mention this term in your answers. (HTP p.73)
	d)		There will be an economic benefit of lower energy bills. (1 mark) There will be an environmental benefit of reduced carbon emissions. (1 mark)	For a system to be intelligent, its programming must allow it to learn from past experience. It will require user input and interaction more often initially, but should progress to needing little or no user interaction as long as user behaviour remains the same. It should respond automatically to data from sensors or other inputs. (HTP p.35) Economic benefits relate to money, but some of these (such as competitive advantage or access to a global marketplace) apply more to a business than to a charity, as in this situation. (HTP pp.75–76)
14	a)		Any one of: - Programming team will be more responsive to changes in client demands - Working code will be developed more quickly (1 mark)	A problem is initially divided into distinct areas and each area is assigned to a separate development team. It is up to each team to develop their assigned area. They may make extensive use of 'prototyping' to try out ideas rather than following rigid designs. One aim is to produce working code quickly. The clients will be consulted and kept informed throughout the development of a project and give feedback. Careful project management is required to ensure the teams come together at the right times to put the project together. (HTP p.20)
	b)		Any one of: - Users can customise the software themselves - Other users may release modifications on the internet (1 mark)	Open source software is software that, when a user obtains the permission/licence to use the software, they are also able to view/access the source program code for the software. Open source software is not always free. However, any users that have access to the code may release modified versions of the program. This is more often related to changes or additions to functionality; the fixing of bugs is more often released as an update/patch by the software development company that created the program. (HTP pp.65–66)

Question			Answer	Hint
	c)		User guide – will explain how to use the program. (1 mark) Technical guide – will explain how to install/run the program OR will contain the system requirements for the program. (1 mark)	While it is true that there may be other documentation also produced (e.g. a licence agreement) the two descriptions listed are the only ones that SQA have accepted in the past. (HTP p.19)
	d)		Any number less than zero – because this is exceptional data that the program should not accept. (1 mark) Zero – because this is extreme data on the boundary of what should be accepted. (1 mark)	The order of your answer isn't important as long as the correct explanation follows each answer. A good test plan will test normal, extreme and exceptional data. Only normal data is present in the table given in the question. (HTP p.13)
	e)		Line 3: `SET max TO numberarray[0]` OR `SET max TO 0` Lines 7, 8, 9: `IF number > max THEN` `SET max TO number` `END IF` (1 mark for Line 3 and Line 8 correct) (1 mark for Line 7 and Line 9 correct)	This is a version of the find maximum standard algorithm. Variations in the language/wording of your answer from the answer given here will still be accepted, as long as the meaning is the same as that given here. Forgetting to end the IF is a frequent mistake. (HTP p.10)
15	a)		Any two of: ■ File management/FMS (1 mark) – locates files on memory card/ ensures sufficient space on hard drive/ allocates space on hard drive/updates file access table/ensures existing files are not overwritten (1 mark) ■ Input–output management/I/O management (1 mark) – handles communication with card reader (1 mark) ■ Memory management/MMS (1 mark) – ensures sufficient space in main memory to handle transfer process/ allocates space in main memory for transfer process/ensures data in main memory is not overwritten (1 mark) ■ Resource allocation (1 mark) – allocates processor time/hard disk access/card reader access to the transfer process (1 mark) ■ Interpreting User Commands/Command Language Interpreter (1 mark) – receives the input from the user and recognises this as the command to begin the file transfer (1 mark)	When asking about functions of an operating system (OS), the questions usually feature a scenario as this one does, rather than asking about a specific function of the OS. It is important to relate your answer to the scenario as well as showing that you have the technical knowledge about the functions of the OS that you have chosen. You must name two functions and give a corresponding correct technical explanation related to the situation to get all 4 marks here.

Question			Answer	Hint
	b)		Any one of: ■ Photographs do not have distinct/separate shapes, which are required for vector storage ■ Vector storage does not allow for individually coloured pixels, which are required to represent a photograph (1 mark)	It is best to give a detailed answer even in 1-mark questions like part (b), to be sure of gaining the mark. Vector graphics are stored using text to represent objects and attributes, whereas bitmap files are stored using a binary colour code for each pixel. *(HTP pp.24–25)*
	c)		Any two of: ■ Can scale without loss of quality/resolution independent ■ Objects can be layered ■ Lower file size/takes less time to transmit ■ Attributes can be edited (2 marks)	
16	**a)**		Any one of: ■ Date ■ Time ■ Script attached to text box/search button (1 mark)	The date and time will be different for each user depending on their location in the world, so must be accessed locally. The search will initially be handled by a client-side script, though that will then initiate a query of the database of products. *(HTP pp.60–61)*
	b)		Any one of: ■ User's name ■ Recommended designs (1 mark)	The user's name has come from the server-side database of user details. That same database will contain details of past activities that have been used to query the server-side database of products in order to show the recommended designs. *(HTP pp.60–61)*
	c)		The Style Printing site has stored a tracking cookie on the device, (1 mark) which the website providing the adverts has accessed. (1 mark)	Tracking cookies are text files that contain information about browsing habits, such as the website visited.
	d)		Any one of: ■ Include a facility to read aloud text on the page ■ Increase font size ■ Change colour scheme to ensure contrast between text and background colours ■ Icons supplemented with auditory feedback (1 mark)	Your answer must be something that can be done by the owners of the website, not by the user on their device. *(HTP p.54)*

Question			Answer	Hint
	e)		The data is encrypted on the user's device using Style Print's public key (1 mark) and the data is decrypted at the destination using Style Print's private key. (1 mark)	This form of encryption involves two algorithms for encryption/decryption. If you encrypt using one, you can decrypt using the other, and vice versa. One algorithm is therefore released to the public as the public key – users can encrypt using this algorithm. The second algorithm that could decrypt the data is kept secret – as a private key. So only the one who released the public key can decrypt data encrypted by that public key – it is decrypted through the use of the private key. (HTP p.70)
17	a)		Any two of: ■ Prototypes allow the client to see what the finished product may look like ■ Client can clarify/change requirements during development ■ A working version of the app can be made available (to customers) more quickly (2 marks)	A prototype is a working version of part of the product produced at an early stage in the development process. (HTP p.20)
	b)		Low level language programs are not portable (1 mark) so Malala could not easily transfer an app created on her desktop to run on a mobile device OR because the low level language will refer directly to components of the desktop's processor. (1 mark)	Low level languages use mnemonics. These are short text codes that mean something in English, but the meaning can be difficult to work out, e.g. one way an IF might be implemented could be with the mnemonic 'JNE', which means 'jump not equal to'. The mnemonic will be used along with references to processor registers or components, which is why low-level instructions are not portable to other processor types. (HTP p.1)
	c)		Use an emulator (1 mark) to simulate the smartphone's software and hardware. (1 mark)	An emulator will use software to act not only like another operating system but also the processor (including components such as registers, ALU, control unit), cache, memory and other hardware of another device. A virtual machine only simulates another operating system but does not simulate hardware. (HTP p.32)

Question			Answer	Hint
	d)	(i)	Any two of: ■ Code would be less readable/harder to maintain (as the flow of data is less clear) ■ Possibility of clashes between variable names ■ Code cannot be easily reused/less portable/modular ■ Greater impact or load on main memory (2 marks)	The name a parameter is given inside a subprogram does not have to be the same as the name given when the variable is in use in the main program or other subprograms (as long as the order and data type of the parameters are the same, the actual names can be different). This means code can be reused (or included in a module library) with no change. When a variable is no longer needed by the program, it is no longer passed as a parameter. The main memory that stored that variable can be released to use for other data. *(HTP pp.7–8)*
		(ii)	Making an extra copy of the array (1 mark) would waste processor time OR would use up main memory. (1 mark)	When passing a variable/array by reference, the subprogram is given the address of the original variable/array in the main memory and so can access and change it. When passing by value, the program makes a copy of the variable/array and will then pass in the address of the copy. Any changes then will not affect the original data, but more main memory and processor time is used when passing by value. *(HTP pp.7–8)*
	e)		Functions return a value. (1 mark) Plus any one of: ■ Procedures perform a list of commands ■ Procedures may change multiple variables ■ Procedures may not change any variables ■ Procedures change variables through parameters (1 mark)	Functions can be pre-defined (including by the creators of the programming language) or user-defined (created by a *programmer* using the language – NOT a user). Variables passed into a function are called 'arguments'. Functions are called using SET, for example to call the LEN function: `SET length TO LEN(name)` The name variable is the argument in this example. *(HTP p.7)*

Question			Answer	Hint
18	a)		Ensure the embedded CPU has multiple cores (1 mark) in order to process simultaneous inputs from sensors/user. (1 mark) OR Ensure sufficient main memory is present (1 mark) to store multiple concurrent/ simultaneous processes. (1 mark)	Multiprogramming is the ability of a system to service multiple processes simultaneously. Multicore processors and sufficient RAM are required to do this. As with all Higher answers, make sure to refer to the situation given in the question.
	b)		Any two of: ■ The system could result in greater fuel efficiency, burning less fossil fuel ■ Internal heating/cooling of the car could be more efficient, wasting less energy ■ More older cars may be scrapped, which could mean more waste in landfill ■ Bernard's system may tempt customers to buy this petrol-powered car rather than a more environmentally friendly electric or hybrid car, which would burn less fossil fuel (2 marks)	These questions require you to show both technical knowledge and common sense. Make sure to provide a lot of detail to be certain of gaining the available marks. (HTP p.76)
	c)		1 Address of instruction placed on address bus 2 Read line (on control bus) is activated 3 Contents of location (instruction) transferred to a register along data bus 4 Instruction decoded/executed (3 marks for all four steps in the correct order) (2 marks for three steps in the correct order OR four steps in incorrect order) (1 mark for two steps in the correct order OR three steps in incorrect order) (0 marks for any other response)	There is no need to mention specific registers such as Memory Address Register, Memory Data Register, Program Counter or Instruction Register. However, you will not be marked down for using these terms correctly. It is important to memorise the steps of the fetch–execute cycle as this kind of question appears fairly often. (HTP p.29)

Question			Answer	Hint
	d)		Users are given set tasks to perform in the car under a set scenario. (1 mark) Observation of performance of users/eye tracking/thinking aloud. OR Feedback is given to developers. (1 mark)	The set tasks and scenarios will allow the developers to target parts of the system to see how they perform under usability testing. Usability testing is a way to see how easy a program or website is to use by testing it with real users. They are asked to complete set tasks while they are being observed by a researcher to see where the users encounter problems. The observed results are fed back to the development team to improve the final version.

Practice Paper B

Section 1

(Where appropriate, hints contain the page number of the relevant corresponding material from *How To Pass Higher Computing Science* by Greg Reid, published by Hodder Gibson. See www.hoddereducation.co.uk for details.)

Question			Answer	Hint
1			-2048 to $+2047$ OR -2^{12-1} to $(2^{12-1}) - 1$ OR 1000 0000 0000 to 0111 1111 1111 (1 mark for upper limit) (1 mark for lower limit)	Two's complement allows storage of both positive and negative numbers. The total number of possible numbers that can be stored with 12 bits is 2^{12}, which is 4096 possible numbers. With two's complement, half of those possible numbers will be negative, so the lower limit is -2048. One of the possible numbers is zero. So, there are only 2047 possible positive integers. This means the upper limit is 2047.
2			Earlier stages are revisited (1 mark) after new information has been gained at a later stage in the process. (1 mark)	The term 'iterative' means that a process repeats. While it can be tempting to explain the iterative nature of the software development process by using an example, any example should be sure to include the key points given here. One example of this could be that a logic error is found at the testing stage, therefore the earlier design stage and implementation stage are revisited to correct the error due to the information gained from the testing stage. *(HTP p.17)*
3			Sample depth $\times 2 \times 60 \times 48\,000 = 11\,250$ Kb Sample depth $\times 2 \times 60 \times 48\,000 = 92\,160\,000$ bits Sample depth $= 92\,160\,000/5\,760\,000$ bits Sample depth $= 16$ bits (or 2 bytes) (2 marks for four correct values OR 1 mark for three correct values in first line) (1 mark for converting to correct units)	The formula for uncompressed audio file size is: Size (bits) = sample rate (Hz) $\times$ sample depth (bits) $\times$ time (seconds) $\times$ no. of channels 48 kHz is 48 000 Hz Stereo sound has two channels – left and right. There are 8 bits in 1 byte, 1024 bytes in 1 kilobyte and 1024 kilobytes in 1 megabyte. While writing the correct answer with the correct units will get you all 3 marks, it is best to show your working in case you have made a mistake so that you can still pick up some marks. *(HTP p.26)*

Question			Answer	Hint
4			Any two of: ■ Cache stores frequently/recently accessed instructions/data ■ Variables used more than once in the algorithm will be present in cache (examples acceptable) ■ Later instructions in the algorithm could be pre-loaded into cache (no branches/IFs to affect this) (2 marks)	Cache memory is a small amount of static RAM placed on the same chip as the processor. Take care not to say 'closer to the processor' as a reason for using cache as this is not accepted. Cache will store the contents of any recently accessed memory locations, but will also 'look ahead' and pre-fetch what should be the next instruction in the sequence as a program executes. This feature is only of use, however, if the program does not branch due to a condition and require a different instruction to be fetched. *(HTP p.31)*
5			Any one of: ■ Lost revenue from customers being unable to access services ■ Paying staff to fix the fault/ vulnerability (1 mark)	A denial of service attack involves network resources being flooded with irrelevant traffic to impair their normal function. This means that genuine requests from customers cannot get serviced by the system in a reasonable amount of time. *(HTP p.70)*
6	a)		The data is encrypted using the public key. (1 mark)	When asymmetric encryption is used, the customer's system will have a pair of keys, and the company's system will have a pair of keys. The keys in a pair are mathematically related, but one cannot be worked out using the other. The company will release one key to all – this is their public key. Anything encrypted with their public key can then only be decrypted by their private key, so the data is secure. The customer will encrypt data using this public key and send it to the company. The customer will also release one key as a public key. The company can encrypt data using the customer's public key, and then the customer can decrypt that data when they receive it using the customer's private key. *(HTP p.70)*
	b)		The private key is required to decrypt data. (1 mark) OR The private key cannot be determined from the public key. (1 mark)	
7			Any one of: ■ Ergonomic/adaptive keyboard to reduce hand/wrist/muscle strain ■ Webcam for eye tracking ■ Microphone for voice input ■ Foot mouse ■ Sip/suck and puff switch (1 mark)	Other answers may be possible. It is important that your answer is an item of hardware as this is stated in the question. Tips for this kind of question are to fully justify your answer and, if you can, give two answers, in case the marking instructions being used do not cover one of your answers.

Question			Answer	Hint
8			Any two of: ■ Facts and rules are stored within the knowledge base ■ Rules can be used in place of multiple facts ■ Queries make use of pattern matching/heuristic search/breadth-first search/depth-first search ■ Uses recursion (2 marks)	Declarative languages are used to create an artificial intelligence system. The knowledge of the system is stored in the knowledge base using facts and rules. Recursion is when a rule calls itself. The knowledge base can be queried to see what the system knows. *(HTP p.3)*
9	a)		`RECORD songdetails IS {STRING title, STRING artist, INTEGER highest chart position}` (1 mark for an obvious record structure with a name) (1 mark for all fields with correct data types)	A record allows a set of variables, with different types, to be named and organised under one data structure. This answer defines that a record called `songdetails` exists, but no instances of the record have been created yet. All text in capitals in the answer here is required exactly as shown. The names (in lower case) were not stated in the question, so just have to be sensible. *(HTP p.7)*
	b)		Any one of: ■ `DIM songCollection[4999] as songdetails` ■ `DECLARE songCollection AS ARRAY OF songdetails INITIALLY [ ] * 4999` ■ `Create variable songCollection[4999] of data type songdetails` (1 mark for array with value) (1 mark for data type from record created in part (a))	As you can see from the answers given, the ideas are more important than the strict syntax of the answer. Be sure to use whichever name you used in your answer to part (a) as a data type for a variable/array with a new name not seen yet in your paper. In this example, the variable/array has been named `songCollection`. Be sure to indicate the array size in square brackets. *(HTP p.7)*
10			ASCII takes up less storage. (1 mark)	Unicode uses 16 bits per character so can store 2^{16} (65 536) characters. ASCII only uses 7 bits per character so can only store 2^7 (128) characters. With ASCII the 8th bit is used as a check digit to take it up to 8 bits. *(HTP p.23)*

Section 2

Question			Answer	Hint
| **11** | **a)** | **(i)** | ```
SET found TO false
SET index TO 0
REPEAT
    IF name(index) = target_
    name THEN
        SET found TO true
        SET target_sold TO
        sold(index)
    END IF
SET index TO index + 1
UNTIL index = 7 OR found = true
IF found THEN
    SEND "The... of" &
    target_name & "was" &
    target_sold TO DISPLAY
ELSE
    SEND "That type is not
    in the list" TO DISPLAY
END IF
``` (1 mark for two correct settings of Boolean (line 1, line 5)) (1 mark for correctly initialising index and incrementing index (line 2, line 8)) (1 mark for use of correct conditional loop (line 3, line 9)) (1 mark for first `IF` statement with the correct condition and `END IF`) (1 mark for assigning a variable to sold(index) within the first `IF`) (1 mark for second `IF` statement with the correct condition and `END IF`) (1 mark for outputs to screen (both `SEND... TO DISPLAY`) | This is a version of the Linear Search standard algorithm. Other structures of this solution are possible. *(HTP pp.7, 10)* |
| | | **(ii)** | ```
SET total TO 0
FOR index FROM 0 TO 7 DO
    IF sold(index) >= 30 THEN
        SET total TO total + 1
    END IF
END FOR
SEND total & "types of tea
sold 30 or more packs this
month" TO DISPLAY
``` (1 mark for correct IF with END IF) (1 mark for incrementing total within the IF) | This is a version of the Count Occurrences standard algorithm. This algorithm will use a fixed loop to traverse the array and keep a running total of entries that meet the condition. *(HTP p.11)* |

Question			Answer	Hint
	b)	(i)	Allocates main memory for the process (1 mark)	The functions of the operating system are: ■ Interpreting user commands – receives input from the user and works out what instruction has been given ■ Memory management – allocates memory to processes, and marks areas of memory as 'free' when processes are finished with them ■ File management – uses the file directory/access table to store the virtual location of a file (in the folder hierarchy) and the physical location of a file (on disk); will mark disk locations as 'free' if data there is deleted ■ Input/output management – handles communication to and from all peripheral devices ■ Resource allocation – prioritises and allocates use of system resources (e.g. access to a device) to different processes ■ Process management – each core can only work on one process at a time; this function of the OS determines which process runs on which core and which have to wait to be processed ■ Error reporting – generates interrupts if an error is detected
		(ii)	Any one of: ■ Identifies a free space on backing storage to store the file ■ Updates file directory/access table (1 mark)	
	c)	(i)	49 (1 mark)	A trace table is a paper and pencil exercise following a set of data through a program and noting how each variable changes at different points in the program. If the value of a variable is different from the expected value, an error has occurred. (HTP pp.12–13)
		(ii)	65 (1 mark)	
	d)		The program tries to access an array element that does not exist (array out of bounds execution error). (1 mark) Plus any one of: ■ Use a variable/parameter to store the size of the array ■ Change the number 7 to END OF LIST ■ Use a function to get the size of the array ■ Use a conditional loop and loop until end of list ■ Change 7 to 6 (line 2) (1 mark)	It is good programming practice to avoid numeric constants in your program where possible. Declaring these as variables instead at the beginning of your program means that should a change be necessary, only one change needs to be made. However, in this situation, there are several solutions that give the desired flexibility, as shown. An execution error is one that occurs while the program is running. (HTP p.12)

Question			Answer	Hint
	e)		Can learn from the trends of what hours the desktop is not in use (1 mark) and automatically shut down OR put into energy-saving mode. (1 mark) OR Can use geolocation on the smartphone (1 mark) to put the desktop into energy-saving mode OR shut it down when the user is not close by. (1 mark) OR User can use app on phone to remotely (1 mark) start up/shut down/use energy-saving mode on the desktop. (1 mark)	Most definitions of an intelligent system would include some form of independent learning by the system based on the data it has gathered. An example showing an automatic action based on previous user behaviour is the best way to show your understanding of the operation of an intelligent system within a context. *(HTP p.35)*
12	a)		Category Product Manufacturer Exporter (3 marks)	For two tables to have a relationship, one of the tables must contain a field that is a foreign key, i.e. the primary key from the other table. Whichever table contains the foreign key is on the 'many' side of a relationship with the table for which that field is the primary key. The answer given here is to the standard required by SQA in 2016–17. However, a more detailed version is likely to be required after changes are made to the course. *(HTP pp.40–41)*

	b)	(i)	`Product.name`
			`Product.Product ID`
			`Product.Description`
			`Manufacturer.Name`
			`Category.Current discount`
			(1 mark for three correct tables)
			(1 mark for five correct fields)
			(1 mark for correctly relating fields to tables)
				Take care to use the field names as given in the description of the database, not those that appear on the screenshot of the web page as those labels are often different. *(HTP p.43)*

		(ii)	`Product.Product ID = 0042` (1 mark)	This is the only entry shown on the query result that is guaranteed to be unique – the shop may sell 'soor plooms' from a number of different manufacturers, so the product name is not an appropriate answer here. *(HTP p.43)*

Question			Answer	Hint

	c)		`<script>`
			`function mouseOver()`
			`{document.`
			`getElementById("dani").`
			`style.color = "blue";}`
			`</script>`
			(1 mark for opening and closing script tags)
			(1 mark for function `mouseOver`)
			(1 mark for document. `getElementById("dani")`)
			(1 mark for `.style.color = "blue"`)
				The HTML h1 element in the question has already been named 'dani', so be sure to use this name. The inclusion of `onmouseover = "mouseOver()"` ensures that the `mouseOver()` function will be called when the pointer moves over the relevant text – your answer need only show what happens within that function. Be sure to spell 'color' in the US way.
				(HTP p.60)

	d)		`<meta name = "keywords"`
			`content = "Scottish,Canada">`
			(1 mark for `"keywords"`)
			(1 mark for `"Scottish,Canada"`)
				Meta tags can be used for a number of purposes. It is important that the tags contain the correct attribute to match with the reason you are using the tag. Here the attribute 'name' is used to indicate that the tag contains keywords followed by the 'content' attribute to specify what those keywords are.
				(HTP p.49)

	e)		Mail services, where emails (and attachments) are stored on servers on the internet, would save local storage capacity. OR meaning emails could be accessed from multiple locations/devices. OR Software updates provided by servers on the internet for Dani's devices. (1 mark) Plus any one of: ■ Device updates can be applied simultaneously ■ Device updates can be scheduled for a convenient time (e.g. at night) ■ Cloud service will be responsible for ensuring that it is the latest update that is installed (1 mark)	Cloud-based services mean that a third party is responsible for aspects such as maintenance of servers, security of data and replacement of storage devices. *(HTP p.67)*

Question			Answer	Hint
13	a)		left OR back (1 mark) An actual parameter is a variable in use in the program that calls the subprogram/function/procedure. OR A copy of an actual parameter can be created and sent in to a subprogram/function/procedure. OR A pointer to the actual parameter can be sent in to a subprogram/function/procedure. (1 mark)	The actual parameters are created within the part of the program that goes on to call the subprogram or function. These variables can be passed into the subprogram by value or by reference. If an actual parameter is passed in by value, the formal parameter will be a copy of the actual parameter that will only exist for the life of the subprogram, and have no effect on the original variable (i.e. the actual parameter). If an actual parameter is passed by reference then the formal parameter will contain a pointer to the actual parameter and any change made to the formal parameter will in fact change the actual parameter. Passing by value or reference allows the programmer to control the flow of data. *(HTP p.8)*
	b)	(i)	8 (1 mark)	The second IF is wrongly placed inside the first IF, so if the hours_hired is not less than one, the second IF is never tested. However, if hours_hired is less than one, the second IF ensures that the higher charge of 8 overwrites the lower charge of 5.
		(ii)	Change line 7 to ELSE IF hours_hired <= 2 THEN. (1 mark)	
	c)		Execution of the program will pause at a specified line of code. (1 mark) The programmer can compare values of variables with expected values. (1 mark)	There are two ways to pause the program mid-execution to check if the variables contain the data the tester believes that they should. Breakpoints are set on a specific line of code, so the program will pause when that line has been executed. Watchpoints are set on a particular variable, so that the program can be set to pause either whenever that variable is accessed or whenever that variable is changed. *(HTP p.13)*
	d)		By value (1 mark) as the function does not change the value of the variable. (1 mark)	Parameters are passed by reference when the subprogram has to be able to change the variable. Passing by value creates a copy of the variable and sends the copy into the subprogram where the subprogram should not change the original variable. *(HTP p.8)*

Question			Answer	Hint
	e)		`Hours_hired` within the function is a local variable. (1 mark)	A local variable is one that is not passed as a parameter and is instead only valid in the subprogram it appears within. Use of local variables allows variables of the same name in different modules without affecting others. Also using local variables makes a program more modular as parts can be developed in isolation by different programmers, or more easily transferred between programs with little or no change. Local variables are more efficient as memory assigned to a local variable becomes available once the function is ended. *(HTP p.7)*
14	a)		Any two of: <ul><li>Can test with a specific user group/novice/expert</li><li>Can assign tasks to test certain areas of the site</li><li>Can receive feedback to improve the user's experience</li></ul>(2 marks)	Usability testing is a way to see how easy a program or website is to use by testing it with real users. They are asked to complete set tasks while they are being observed by a researcher to see where the users encounter problems. The observed results are fed back to the development team to improve the final version.
	b)		Any one of: <ul><li>Sort Results By</li><li>Select View</li><li>Your Basket</li></ul>(1 mark)	Take care with these questions as there are a lot of items on the page that would be incorrect due to not requiring any scripting. Just because an item is not generated with server-side scripting, does not automatically mean that it uses client-side scripting. The 'Go' button does not require scripting to operate, but will initiate the search, which is server-side scripting. The underlined text will link to another page, but scripting is not required for a simple hyperlink. The same is true of selecting Football, Rugby, Cricket or Other. The correct choices all make use of the database records that have already been sent to the client computer by the server. *(HTP pp.60–61)*
	c)		Any two of: <ul><li>A connection with the database/server is created</li><li>Data from the web page form is captured and used to create the query</li><li>The results that match the criteria are returned to update the web page</li></ul>(2 marks)	PHP scripts are executed on the server and mySQL is used to query the database. The client computer does not see PHP or SQL as the results are sent back as part of an HTML document. *(HTP pp.60–61)*

Question			Answer	Hint
d)	**(i)**		Data could be lost if a fault occurs between the weekly full backups. (1 mark)	It is necessary to state how often your selected backup will be used. That is what makes it a backup schedule. The full backup backs up all data regardless of whether or not it has changed, so this is the most time consuming, uses most system resources and most backing storage capacity. The differential always saves the changes since the last full backup, so any previous differential backup data that is saved is not needed any more. This is more time consuming than incremental but could save storage capacity if the previous differential backups are deleted. Incremental backup saves all the changes since the last backup of any type so it can be done quite quickly but can lead to a large number of smaller backup files, potentially some of which are storing data that is not needed any more.
	(ii)		Use a differential backup (1 mark) to save all changes since the last full backup (1 mark) hourly/daily. (1 mark) OR Use an incremental backup (1 mark) to save all changes since the last backup of any type (1 mark) hourly/daily. (1 mark)	
	e)		With a public cloud the data is stored securely on the servers of a third party. (1 mark) A hybrid cloud stores some data on a public cloud, but other data is stored securely on servers owned by Alford Kits/ the company that owns the data. (1 mark)	Cloud services all store data securely. They will use firewalls and encryption to ensure this. An authorised user can log in to any of the cloud services remotely with a username and password. Public cloud services are provided by an outside company, most likely to many customers, with all the data kept to separate areas of the cloud for each customer. A private cloud is when a company operates their own cloud services instead. A hybrid cloud is when a company chooses to use a combination of these. Don't be confused: public cloud storage still requires log-on by a user with the correct username and password to access data. (HTP p.67)

Question			Answer	Hint
	f)	(i)	The colour (code) of the affected/relevant pixels would be changed. (Pixels where the oval has moved from are changed from black to white; pixels where the oval has moved to are changed from white to black.) (1 mark)	Vector graphics are stored as text. The text is the list of objects (shapes) and their attributes. Attributes include line colour, fill colour, coordinates and the layer the shape is on. Adding a new object adds more text to the file, so increases file size. The system uses the text to produce the image; it is not stored at a set resolution, so the resolution is determined by the available hardware – scaling will not lead to pixilation. This is known as resolution independence.
		(ii)	Attributes/coordinates of the shape will be changed (can be done by dragging the shape or editing the text of the file). (1 mark)	
	g)	(i)	The new designs have a higher file size (1 mark) as new shapes/instructions/attributes have been added. (1 mark)	Bitmapped graphics are stored using a colour code for each pixel in the image. To move or remove an object involves changing the colour code for the relevant pixels. These images are saved at a set resolution when created. *(HTP pp.24–25)*
		(ii)	No change to file size (1 mark) as the colour of existing pixels has been changed but no new pixels have been added. (1 mark)	
15	a)	(i)	Stores a colour code that repeats in the graphic (1 mark) and stores the number of consecutive pixels that have that colour code. (1 mark)	Run length encoding is lossless compression – there is no loss of quality. It is used where a number of pixels in a row have the same colour. The colour code for that colour is stored, along with the number of pixels in a row that have that exact colour. *(HTP p.56)*
		(ii)	Areas of similar colour are set to the same colour. (1 mark) This means there will be more repetitions of a colour code within the graphic. (1 mark)	Discrete cosine transform is a lossy compression method where the image is divided into blocks of 8×8 pixels. A mathematical equation is applied to each block. The resulting effect is that there are fewer available colours because areas of similar colour are set to the same colour. Fewer possible colour codes can then aid RLE or LZW compression. *(HTP p.57)*

Question			Answer	Hint
b)	**(i)**		Interframe compression saves the differences/changes between frames. (1 mark) File size is smaller for the speech because i-frames will be smaller for a video with little movement. OR File size is larger for the dance because i-frames will be larger for a video with more movement. OR File size is larger for the dance because more key frames will be needed in a video with lots of movement. (1 mark)	Intraframe compression compresses each frame, perhaps using DCT and/or RLE as described above. The first part of interframe compression involves saving an initial frame called a key frame. Perhaps one of these would be saved each time the camera angle changes or a new scene begins, as that frame will then have little resemblance to the preceding frames. The second part of interframe compression involves saving subsequent frames, called i-frames, where only the changes from the frame before are saved. The i-frames are saved in this way until the next major change, when a new key frame would then be saved. *(HTP p.58)*
		(ii)	The frame rate was too low when capturing the video.	The frame rate is the number of frames captured per second. If frames are not captured often enough, a lot of movement may have happened between captures, causing playback to look jerky and unnatural. *(HTP pp.26–27)*
c)			The text 'Welcome To' will be centred and coloured green. On the next line, the text 'Boris Romanov' will be centred, coloured blue, double the size of the text on the first line. On the third line, the text 'Videography' will be centred, coloured green and the same size text as the first line. (1 mark for correct colours) (1 mark for correct alignment and size) (1 mark for correctly identifying when text is on a new line)	The CSS shown first is internal CSS that sets up that paragraph (indicated by the <p> tag) should be centre-aligned with a text colour of green. This formatting applies in line 1 'Welcome To'. Line 2 has some inline CSS that supersedes (replaces) the internal CSS from the head section. So the size is changed for this text, and the colour is also changed. However, the inline CSS makes no mention of alignment, so the alignment of the original internal CSS rule still applies (centre-aligned). Line 3 has no inline CSS so the internal CSS rule still applies to this text. Every pair of <p> and </p> is indicating a new paragraph, so appears on a new line. *(HTP pp.82–83)*
d)			Proprietary software is produced by a software development company. (1 mark) Proprietary support is provided by the company who produced it. OR Boris may already be familiar with the user interface of proprietary software from previous versions. (1 mark)	Proprietary software often appears in questions involving a comparison with open source software, such as in the 2016 paper. Many of the advantages that you may think of for one of these types of software can actually apply to both, so take care, e.g. both types can be free and both types are likely to benefit from prompt updates. Advantages of open source include that it provides support via a community of users and developers, and open source code can be edited. *(HTP p.65)*

C

Practice Paper C

Section 1

(Where appropriate, hints contain the page number of the relevant corresponding material from *How To Pass Higher Computing Science* by Greg Reid, published by Hodder Gibson. See www.hoddereducation.co.uk for details.)

Question			Answer	Hint
1			116 (1 mark)	'Denary' is a name for the base 10, or decimal, number system that you are used to. Invert the bits to get 01110011 Add 1 to get 01110100 Converting, this is 4 + 16 + 32 + 64 = 116 When adding 1, be careful that when you carry a 1 to the next column you place a 0 in the column you're in, i.e. in binary 011 + 001 = 100 When converting, remember that the place values of the bits begin with 1 at the right-most place, and double each time. So from the right, with 8 bits, the values are 1, 2, 4, 8, 16, 32, 64, 128. *(For an alternative method, see HTP pp.22–23)*
2			Autumn OR Winter OR Spring OR Summer (1 mark) A variable/a parameter/data that must be passed in to a function for the function to operate. (1 mark)	Most functions require some information to be able to do their job, for example the LEN ( ) function will return the length of a string that is passed in to the function as an argument, such as SET length to LEN (name). *(HTP p.24)*

Question			Answer	Hint
3			The possible precision will increase. (1 mark) The possible range will decrease. (1 mark)	The mantissa part of the floating point number is responsible for the precision/accuracy of the number. The number of bits for this has increased from 8 to 16, so the number can be more precise. The exponent part of the floating point number is responsible for the range of possible numbers that can be stored. The number of bits for this has decreased from 24 to 16, so the number cannot have as wide a range as before. *(HTP p.23)*
4			Any two of: ■ Instructions are executed in the order in which they appear ■ Programs have defined start and end points ■ Groups of instructions can be repeated using fixed or conditional loops ■ Branching is possible within the programs, using conditional/IF statements ■ Modular as sets of instructions can be contained within procedures/subroutines ■ Data can be passed between procedures/subroutines through parameter passing (2 marks)	Procedural languages are designed to allow programmers to create programs that follow a logical order. SQA have not asked an examination question specifically about these as yet, so be sure to include as much information as you can in your answer to be sure of gaining the available marks. *(HTP p.2)*
5			Lesley will be able to sell the game to more customers. (1 mark)	If a program or information system is portable then it can be run on a computer system other than the one it was designed on, with little or no change. This means Lesley will attract customers other than those who own only a certain type of computer. *(HTP p.65)*
6			Any two of: ■ Instructions 3/4 will already be (pre-loaded) in cache, i.e. a cache hit will occur ■ Data in variable `password` will already be in cache, improving access time/instruction time ■ Instruction 4 may never be reached, so pre-loading may have no effect (2 marks)	Computer systems will pre-load cache with the upcoming instructions to make fetching them quicker than from slower main memory. However, this can be of no use if the program branches (using an IF). Recently accessed data is also stored in cache. Cache need only be checked for data when attempting to read data from main memory – data stored in registers is already inside the processor. Registers are faster access memory than cache. *(HTP p.31)*

Question			Answer	Hint
7			Any two of: Privacy settings should allow users to: ■ control who can see what they post ■ control who can see their profile ■ control who can see specific personal information, e.g. date of birth, location, contact details. (2 marks)	Social media sites must allow users to configure their privacy settings so that the users can protect themselves and their information from being accessed by anyone without their permission. SQA have not asked an examination question specifically about these as yet, so be sure to include as much information as you can in your answer to be sure of gaining the available marks. (HTP p.76)
8			`<link rel = "stylesheet" type = "text/css" href = "webstyle.css">` (1 mark for `link`) (1 mark for `type`)	This must be placed in the head section of the HTML to apply the styling contained within the external stylesheet to the web page. Be careful to include 'css' at the end of the filename. (HTP p.50)
9	a)		Any one of: ■ Increase font size ■ High resolution displays ■ Icons supplemented with auditory feedback ■ Screen magnifying software ■ Screen reader software ■ Speech recognition software ■ Braille display/keyboard (1 mark)	For this kind of question, be sure to justify your answer within any context given in the question. You may wish to give two points for each to be sure of gaining the mark available.
	b)		Any one of: ■ Subtitles/closed caption/text transcript ■ Replace system sounds like beeps with visual notifications and captioned text ■ Use visual warnings whenever the computer generates a sound ■ Noise cancelling headphones (1 mark)	
10			Weather website may go down or move the content on their site, so that the link is broken. (1 mark) Weather website may send incorrect information. (1 mark)	Dynamic content is content that continually changes without user interaction. In this case, that content is provided by an external source that the zoo has no control over. This means errors can occur that the zoo can do little to prevent, such as those listed. (HTP p.51)

Question			Answer	Hint
11			Stores repeated patterns of data in a 'dictionary' file. (1 mark) Stores a code to match these repeating blocks in the data file. (1 mark)	Lempel Ziv Welch compression looks for repeating patterns within the data. When a repeating pattern is found it is stored in a dictionary file, along with a shorter binary code to identify it. When the pattern appears in the image, the data file for the image will store the shorter 'lookup' code rather than the full pattern code. However, the data file cannot reproduce the image without the dictionary file. This is a lossless compression technique. E.g: If this was being used to compress an 800×800 bitmap of a chess board, it would notice that each row of pixels has only one of two possible patterns. Either the pattern of 100 white pixels then 100 black pixels four times, or the pattern of 100 black pixels then 100 white pixels four times. So the dictionary file would store '0' and the first pattern, then '1' and the second pattern. This means the data file would only store one bit for each row of pixels in the image. *(HTP pp.56–57)*

Question			Answer	Hint
| 12 | a) | | ```
OPEN FILE "stats.txt"
FOR counter FROM 0 TO 31 DO
    RECEIVE authority(counter).
    name FROM FILE
    RECEIVE authority(counter).
    annual_rainfall FROM FILE
    RECEIVE authority(counter).
    hours_sunshine FROM FILE
    RECEIVE authority(counter).
    average_windspeed FROM FILE
NEXT counter
CLOSE FILE
``` (1 mark for open and close file)<br>(1 mark for correct fixed loop/end loop)<br>(1 mark for correct relation of field name to record name)<br>(1 mark for reading from file using 'counter' correctly to index the array) | Remember: arrays are indexed from zero. Dot notation is often used when referencing attributes of records within programs. However, if you just have `authority.name`, the program wouldn't know which of the authorities you are referring to, so the correct syntax is either `authority(counter).name` or `authority.name(counter)`.<br>*(HTP p.7)* |
| | b) | | Any two of:
■ Jiong's windspeeds are of type real; this function processes windspeeds of type integer
■ This function returns only the number of the highest windspeed, not the name of the authority this corresponds to
■ Jiong's windspeeds are as attributes within an array of records; he cannot pass only the windspeeds as an array into this function as an argument
(2 marks) | The arguments are the parameters passed into a function so that it can do its job. Rebekah's function here expects one argument; an array of integers. Jiong has used an array of records, so the function would have to be changed to accept an array of records. Once this had been done, it could then be further changed to find the name of the authority with the highest average windspeed. |
| 13 | a) | | ```
SET total to 0
FOR entry FROM 0 TO 299 DO
    IF age(entry)<18 THEN
        SET total TO total+1
    END IF
END FOR
SEND total TO DISPLAY
``` (1 mark for initialising total to 0)<br>(1 mark for correct loop/end loop)<br>(1 mark for IF with correct condition and END IF)<br>(1 mark for increment total)<br>(1 mark for displaying total) | This is an example of the count occurrences standard algorithm.<br>*(HTP p.11)* |

Question			Answer	Hint
	b)		Dunton Juniors should obtain a digital certificate for their site. (1 mark) This means that the site is authenticated/issued by a certification authority. OR This means the site is regulated. (1 mark)	Digital certificates are issued by a third party that confirms the identity of a website. The certificate contains the name of the certificate holder, a serial number, expiration dates, a copy of the certificate holder's public key and the digital signature of the certificate-issuing authority. *(HTP p.70)*
	c)		Any one of: ■ Only ask for certain digits from the user ID or PIN ■ Allow input of digits via a drop-down menu using the mouse (1 mark)	Keyloggers track the keys pressed by a user on their keyboard. If only some sensitive data is typed, and that out of order, or better yet not typed at all, then the keylogger will not have the data to send on to a criminal. Antivirus software is not an appropriate answer as only the client could install this on their computer; this is not a precaution that could be taken by Dunton Juniors. *(HTP p.70)*
	d)		Any two of: ■ The URL should include relevant keywords ■ The title of each page should include relevant keywords ■ Meta tags/meta data with appropriate keywords ■ Ensuring there are more links to the site from other sites ■ Keyword loading/stuffing – add more relevant text content to body of web pages (2 marks)	Search engines will use an algorithm to rank pages based on a number of criteria. Due to a lot of sites filling meta tags with keywords, some of which are irrelevant to the site's content, search engines use factors such as the number of external links to a site and the ranking given to the sites that link to the site to help rank results. Results where the keywords appear many times, close together, in the body of the web page will be ranked more highly.
	e)		Different groups/profiles. (1 mark) Different rights/permissions. (1 mark)	Each username on the network can be assigned to the appropriate group. Then permissions are set for each group to give them access rights only to the files/folders that they should see.
	f)		Any one of: ■ If a hacker were to gain access to the network, they cannot access data in offline storage ■ If a virus were to infect the network, it cannot corrupt data in offline storage ■ Physical methods of preventing access to the storage media can be used (1 mark)	Offline storage is when files are stored on backing storage that is not connected to the network. Usually this involves a computer in a locked room for access to this data. Other security measures can be put in place for access to that room, e.g. biometrics such as fingerprint scanners, though this would be a bit extreme in this situation.

Question			Answer	Hint
g)	**(i)**		Quality will have been lost as DCT is lossy compression. (1 mark)	DCT loses data by looking at areas of 8 × 8 pixels and applying a formula. The result means that fewer colours are shown, so data and quality are lost. *(HTP p.57)*
		(ii)	Analogue-to-digital conversion will already have taken place within the digital camera at the time of capture/storage.	An interface is designed to compensate for differences between how a device may operate and how a computer operates. In the past, it was a piece of hardware separate from either, but nowadays it is usually part of the peripheral device. The five functions of an interface are: ■ data format conversion for converting camera signals, e.g. serial to parallel ■ buffering/temporary storage of data in transit between the camera and the computer compensates for differences in speed between the camera and the computer ■ handling of status signals so as to ensure camera data is received correctly ■ voltage conversion so as to change voltage levels of the camera to relevant levels for the computer ■ protocol conversion to ensure camera and computer adhere to the same protocols. Ordinarily data format conversion between analogue and digital might also be relevant, but is not in this case as this is done in the digital camera at the time of capture, not at the time of transfer to a computer. *(HTP p.31)*

Question			Answer	Hint

		(iii)	Any two of:
			
			■ Interpreting user commands (1 mark):
			  ■ receives the input from the user to initiate transfer (1 mark)
			■ File management (1 mark):
			  ■ identifies a free space on backing storage to place photo files (1 mark)
			  OR
			  ■ updates/checks file directory/file access table (1 mark)
			  OR
			  ■ locates files on camera storage (1 mark)
			■ Memory management (1 mark):
			  ■ allocates main memory for process/photos (1 mark)
			■ Input/output management (1 mark):
			  ■ transfers from camera memory to backing storage (1 mark)
			■ Resource allocation/process management (1 mark):
			  ■ managing processes and memory (1 mark)
			■ Error reporting (1 mark):
			  ■ generates an interrupt if there is an error during transfer (1 mark)
				The operating system has seven main functions.
				
				Interpreting user commands processes information entered by the user and converts this to the correct instruction that the user intended to give.
				
				Memory management monitors what areas of main memory (RAM) are available for use and assigns memory to processes.
				
				File management uses a file access table to keep track of the physical location of data on the storage devices and link this to their apparent location within the folders and subfolders that the user sees. It keeps track of free space.
				
				Input/output management ensures that communication with devices takes place.
				
				Resource allocation determines which processes can access which system resources at any given time.
				
				Process management decides which process (or processes if multiple cores are available) will receive processor time.
				
				Error reporting detects errors and generates an interrupt if necessary.

	h)		Any two of: ■ Stores an attempt to predict the frequency of future samples (linear prediction) ■ Stores the difference between what was predicted and what was actually sampled (Golomb-Rice encoding) ■ Applies run length encoding/RLE (2 marks)	This would be particularly effective on human speech as the frequency of one person's voice does not change a great deal across the course of a recording, so the linear prediction would be quite close to the actual samples. Other features of FLAC include that it is open source and that it was designed to be quick to decompress and for fast playback.
14	a)		Any one of: ■ Instructor ID ■ Booking ID (1 mark)	A surrogate key is an extra field added to the database to uniquely identify each record in a database. The field added here is not a required piece of data about the instructor/booking, but is instead extra artificial (made-up) data only so they can have a unique ID. The `Autonumber` field type is often used for this in popular database applications. Your SQA candidate number is an example of a surrogate key.

Question			Answer	Hint
	b)		Instructor ▷──── Resort ────◁ Track Resort ──▽── Booking (1 mark for each correct relationship: Many Instructors to one Resort Many Tracks to one Resort Many Bookings to one Resort)	For two tables to have a relationship, one of the tables must contain a field that is a foreign key, i.e. the primary key from the other table. Whichever table contains the foreign key is on the 'many' side of a relationship with the table for which that field is the primary key. This example is particularly tricky as all the relationships are with the Resort table. A database like this could just as easily be set up with the relationship between Instructor and Booking rather than Instructor and Resort, so be careful not to use your own common sense but stick to checking where the 'FK' text appears. The answer given here is to the standard required by SQA in 2016–17. However, a more detailed version is likely to be required after changes are made to the course. *(HTP pp.40–41.)*
	c)		Add a Boolean-type field to the Booking table. (1 mark)	Boolean fields can only have two values: true or false. On the screen they are normally represented as a check box.
	d)		Set up a form that allows entry of resort name and difficulty. (1 mark) Use the form contents to construct a query (1 mark) on the fields `Resort.Name` and `Track.Difficulty`. (1 mark) Update the screen with the query results. (1 mark)	Forms allow data entry from users only in a restricted way. However, that data must still be made use of to query the database. Be sure to include sufficient detail about all steps to gain all the available marks. *(HTP p.42)*
	e)	**(i)**	Any two of: ■ Data is duplicated across servers so if one goes down the data is still available ■ Data is duplicated across servers so if one is busy another can service the request ■ Requests can be serviced by a physically closer server that will allow faster access (2 marks)	Distributed data storage involves storing the same data on two or more servers in physically separate locations. While this involves duplication of data, which costs more in terms of purchasing storage hardware, there are clear advantages relating to data access.
		(ii)	Any one of: ■ Changes to records may take time to be applied across all relevant servers ■ Connection to other sites may go down, perhaps making some data inaccessible (1 mark)	Office staff concerns will be related to functionality of the database.

Question			Answer	Hint
		(iii)	Any one of: ■ Broadband ■ Optical fibre ■ UTP ■ Copper wire ■ T1-5 ■ DS1-5 leased from a telecom company ■ ISP (1 mark)	Where a network stretches across a large geographical area, it will prove necessary to lease a connection. Satellite links would not be needed for a connection entirely within the UK.
	f)		Create a web-based app rather than a native app. (1 mark) This can then be viewed using any browser (regardless of operating system). (1 mark) OR So that there is no need to install an app for a specific operating system. (1 mark)	Development of different apps for different operating systems is eliminated in the question. Use of emulators is not valid as the question focuses on what Paterson Dirt Moto could do rather than what the users could do. (HTP p.62)
	g)	(i)	Any two of: ■ If a GPS signal indicates that a bike is taking a good deal longer than usual to navigate a track, alert an instructor ■ If a GPS signal indicates that a bike has remained stationary on the track for a certain length of time, alert an instructor ■ If a GPS signal indicates that a bike has left the track, alert an instructor ■ If a GPS signal indicates that a bike is extremely close to another bike, alert an instructor ■ If a GPS signal is lost, alert an instructor of the last known location (2 marks)	Most definitions of an intelligent system would include some form of independent learning by the system based on the data it has gathered. An example showing an automatic action based on previous user behaviour is the best way to show your understanding of the operation of an intelligent system within a context. In this context, the system is learning about the shape of the track and the time users should take to get around it. Various automatic actions can be taken based on input from the GPS sensor meeting certain conditions. (HTP p.35)
		(ii)	Specific processes/instructions/tasks/bikes can be allocated to certain processors/core processors (1 mark) allowing concurrent/simultaneous execution/parallel processing. (1 mark)	Multicore processors allow parallel processing, i.e. multiple processes being serviced simultaneously. With a number of bikes sending simultaneous updates, this is clearly advantageous in this situation. (HTP p.30)

Question			Answer	Hint
15	**a)**		Any two of: ■ Uses English-like words, so it is easier to learn/find errors/create programs ■ Portable as it can easily be transferred between systems other than the one it was designed on with little or no change ■ Translation to machine code is required/necessary (2 marks)	Be sure to include sufficient detail in your answer. *(HTP p.1)*
	b)		Correct Normal test data to be entered (any integer 1–99) with the expectation that this will be accepted. (1 mark) Correct Extreme test data to be entered (0 or 100) with the expectation that this will be accepted. (1 mark) Correct Exceptional test data to be entered (integer less than 0 or integer greater than 100 or real value) with the expectation that this will not be accepted. (1 mark)	A test plan always includes the expected result for an entry. Stating the type of test data (Normal/Extreme/Exceptional) is advised. Extreme is valid data that is right on the edge of a boundary. Exceptional is invalid data. Candidates may be tempted to use a string as an Exceptional entry but it is best to stick to a number to be sure of gaining the mark. *(HTP p.13)*

	c)		```
			FOR index = 0 TO 7
			  IF score(index) = 100 THEN
			    SEND name(index) TO
			    DISPLAY
			  END IF
			NEXT index
			``
			(1 mark for correct fixed loop with END loop)
			(1 mark for IF with correct condition)
			(1 mark for displaying name within the IF)
				This is a version of the linear search standard algorithm. The data given has more than one pupil who has scored 100, so be careful to display the data inside the IF and FOR loop rather than at the end to avoid only showing the last name found.
				(HTP p.10)

Question			Answer	Hint
	d)		Can edit individual pixels. (1 mark)	Bit-mapped graphics work by storing a colour code in binary for each individual pixel, laid out like a 'map' of the screen/image. File types include bmp, jpg, gif and png. Bitmaps usually take up more space than vector graphics. Bitmap packages lose the underlying pixel data when shapes overlap; vector graphics store the shapes separately so overlapping has no loss of data. Bitmap images are created at a set number of pixels, so have a set resolution; vector graphics are used as instructions by the computer to draw the shapes, so vector graphics can be scaled up with no loss of quality. This is called resolution independence. Bitmaps enable you to edit individual pixels. A vector graphic will only allow you to change attributes, e.g. fill colour, fill pattern, line colour, line pattern. Vector graphics require distinct shapes and so are not suitable for photographs. Captured images will be saved as bitmaps. *(HTP pp.24–25)*
16	**a)**		The number of still images captured/stored for one second of video. (1 mark)	Video is represented as a sequence of still frames. The resolution is the number of pixels in a frame; the bit depth is the number of bits per pixel and determines the number of available colours. *(HTP pp.26–27)*
	b)		Large square containing text like 'Preview of video' with label 'Plays video' or similar. (1 mark) Blank area at the bottom with label 'Description entered here' or similar. (1 mark) Three buttons containing appropriate icons with labels like 'Share to social media', 'Quit' and 'Show menu'. (1 mark) Possible solution: 	The user interface is frequently designed through wireframing. In wireframing, a sketch of each screen shown in the program is made, showing the locations of any prompts/output displayed and indicating areas where users will enter input. *(HTP p.47)*

Question			Answer	Hint
	c)	(i)	Problems are broken down into steps. (1 mark) Each step is further broken down until it can be solved in one line of code. (1 mark)	Step-wise refinement is a form of top-down design.
		(ii)	Any one of: ■ Different teams of programmers can be assigned to different tasks/modules at the same time ■ Perhaps some code can be reused due to modular nature of solution, saving development time (1 mark)	Be sure your answer refers to development time. A module is a section of code, such as a method, function or procedure/subroutine. A module library may contain fully coded and documented modules that can be reused in order to reduce development time. (HTP p.7)
	d)		Execution of the program will pause when a specified variable is accessed/changed. (1 mark) The programmer can compare values of variables with expected values. (1 mark)	There are two ways to pause the program mid-execution in order to check if the variables contain the data the tester believes that they should. Breakpoints are set on a specific line of code, so the program will pause when that line has been executed. Watchpoints are set on a particular variable, so that the program can be set to pause either whenever that variable is accessed or whenever that variable is changed.
	e)		The beta testers may find errors that in-house testers have overlooked. (1 mark) The beta testers may generate user interest in the app/smartphone. (1 mark)	In many situations beta testers will also test the software with a variety of operating systems and software and hardware configurations, which can make it more likely that any potential clashes will be found. However, that is not relevant in this situation as all will be testing on the new smartphone. (HTP p.19)
	f)		Any two of: ■ To fix/correct an error/security flaw discovered after release ■ To enable the app to work with a new version of the smartphone's operating system ■ To add a new feature to the app (2 marks)	Maintenance is changing a program after its release. Corrective maintenance is amending a program to fix errors that were not found in pre-release testing. Adaptive maintenance is changing the program to work under new conditions. This could be for a new or upgraded operating system, or could be to work with new hardware. Perfective maintenance is adding new functionality to software. (HTP p.19)

Question		Answer	Hint
g)		Any one of: ■ The user's phone may not have enough main memory ■ The user's phone may not have enough processor speed/cores ■ The app may not be compatible with the older operating system ■ The app may require hardware that is not present in the old smartphone (1 mark)	Compatibility issues are common when trying to run newer versions of software on older devices. The new phone may feature an accelerometer that the old one lacks, or may use an onscreen keyboard via a touchscreen where the old phone had a keypad. (HTP p.62)
h)		Any one of: ■ As it has improved specifications, the new phone may require more power to run, some of which will come from fossil fuels and lead to a greater concentration of carbon dioxide in the atmosphere, contributing to global warming. ■ The new phone may have improved power efficiency, requiring less power to run, some of which will come from fossil fuels and lead to less carbon dioxide than would otherwise have been released by use of the phone, and less of an increase in the greenhouse effect. ■ Phones/materials will require energy for their transportation, some of which will come from fossil fuels and lead to a greater concentration of carbon dioxide in the atmosphere, contributing to global warming. ■ Raw materials may have to be mined, causing unsightly damage to the landscape. ■ Raw materials may have to be mined, requiring energy, some of which will come from fossil fuels and lead to a greater concentration of carbon dioxide in the atmosphere, contributing to global warming. ■ More obsolete phones may be sent to landfill, releasing harmful chemicals into the ecosystem. (1 mark)	Marking instructions in the past for this kind of question have required a lot of detail in order to gain the mark. Be sure to put in as much detail as you can. (HTP p.76)